Love from Cork
Postcards of the City & County

Perry O'Donovan, from west Cork, is an author, book-editor and blogger. A graduate of London's South Bank Polytechnic and the University of Edinburgh, in the 1990s Perry worked on the Darwin Correspondence Project at Cambridge University editing the letters of Charles Darwin, a 33-volume series published by Cambridge University Press. *Santiago, Here I Come!* is his collection of essays on walking to Santiago de Compostela in northwest Spain (2008). His writing has appeared in *The Irish Times*, the *Irish Examiner*, *The Southern Star*, and the *Sunday Independent*. The Wordkern Archive on WordPress.com is Perry's blog (www.wordkern.wordpress.com).

Love from Cork

Postcards of the City & County

Perry O'Donovan

The Collins Press

First published in 2013 by
The Collins Press
West Link Park
Doughcloyne
Wilton, Cork

© Perry O'Donovan 2013

A CIP record for this book is available from the British Library.

ISBN: 978-1848891906

Design and typesetting by Inspire.ie

Printed in Poland by Białostockie Zakłady Graficzne SA

CONTENTS

INTRODUCTION

'DELTIOLOGY' is the term that describes the study and collection of postcards – it is derived from a cluster of Greek words together meaning 'little writing tablet'. If you have not encountered it before it would not be surprising as it was coined only in the 1940s, and did not appear in a dictionary until the 1960s. Even today the term would not be widely disseminated – much less so, for example, than 'philately', its stamp-collecting cousin.

Almost every deltiologist has a category of interest – transportation systems, communication systems, the work of a particular publisher or artist, animals in postcards, children or toys in postcards, religious or political subjects, and so on – infinite possibilities – ballet postcards, castle postcards, sports cards, the shop-fronts of Ulster…you name it and someone somewhere is probably specializing in it.

The most common collecting category, of course, is geographically framed, the town or city or territory in which one lives, or in which one happens to be especially interested. Locations are sometimes then combined with time-periods – New York city postcards from the 1940s and 50s, for example, or postcards posted in Dublin on Bloomsday (the original Bloomsday, 16 June 1904) – and, in turn, place and time may be triangulated with a third dimension: London postcards from the inter-war years featuring motor cars or women's hats or whatever.

Collectors can have a number of areas of interest in harness, which may or may not be inter-connected and/or overlap – John James, for example, one of the two principal collectors featured in this volume, in addition to his collection of Cork postcards, collects cards relating to the Cunard ocean liner *Lusitania* – in its day the world's biggest passenger vessel – torpedoed and sunk by a German U-boat in May 1915 (the *Lusitania* went down 11 miles south of the Old Head of Kinsale with the loss of nearly 1,200 lives).

John James started off collecting postcards of his hometown, Kinsale. As a schoolboy, John had the collecting bug for a little while – collecting railway-related items, including postcards – however, he did not start collecting in a serious way until he retired (most of John James' working life was spent with the British Bank of the Middle East – now part of HSBC group. He retired from the bank in 1986).

"I was very fortunate early on in my collecting career," he says "in meeting at a postcard fair in London an experienced dealer, whose advice was to select a very limited number of subjects to collect, and for whatever reason do not deviate one jot from one's target subjects."

Nevertheless, it was not long before John's geographical area of interest extended to the county boundary – Kinsale simply being too confined an area to make the activity rewarding – "it requires both fortitude and stamina to wade through boxes and boxes of common cards."

He developed his discipline in other ways, however, specializing in cards from the Golden Age of the Picture Postcard, that is, cards produced between the 1890s and the 1920s.

"Financial constraints also impose certain limitations", John adds. Postcards are vastly more expensive than they were 25 years ago when he started collecting. In the 1980s, £5 would have been an *enormous* sum to pay for a postcard. However, in the late 1990s, for instance, John was at an auction in Dublin at which a postcard of Lord Carbery landing an aeroplane at the Cork Show Grounds sold for £117 (Irish punts) – this, in fairness, was exceptional. John had been bidding for the Lord Carbery card but dropped out of the competition once it started to become, in his view, silly money.

To date, John has nearly 2,000 cards in his collection, with Kinsale (158), Cork city (299), and Queenstown-Cobh (105) making up the three largest sub-sets.

"My Holy Grail is to obtain a card of Kinsale Railway Station", he says. "I know a card of it exists – with a detachment of soldiers marching away from it – but I have never seen it."

Mischievously, in summing up, he says, "I would say that collecting picture postcards is not so much a hobby as a *disease*!"

"Postcarditis" has long been recognised as a feverish and pitiable condition – the following is from the *American Magazine* from as long ago as 1906:

> "Postal carditis and allied collecting manias are working havoc among the inhabitants of the United States. The germs of these maladies, brought to this country in the baggage of tourists and immigrants, escaped quarantine regulations, and have propagated with amazing rapidity…
>
> "By far the worst development of the prevailing pests is postal carditis, which affects the heart, paralyzes the reasoning faculties, and abnormally increases the nerve. It had its origin in Germany twenty years ago, but did not assume dangerous proportions there until 1897. Sporadic cases of it were observed in the United States and the year 1900 saw the malady rapidly spread from one center of infection to another. It seems only yesterday that postal cards were on view almost entirely at hotels which were patronized exclusively by foreigners or in little dingy shops on Third Avenue, or on the remote East side.
>
> "It often happens that collectors . . . have not enough friends to increase their hoards in a normal manner. Hundreds of them haunt establishments where the causes of their besetting sin are exposed for sale, select such as strike their fancy, stamp them and mail them to their own addresses. . . .
>
> "These monstrosities [albums of postcards] are often bestowed on the center table in the parlor, and about the only thing that can be said for them is that they crowd off the plush thesaurus of family celebrities."

Meanwhile, in the west of the county, on weekends and during school holidays, Adrian Healy worked in a little seaside village shop. The shop ceased trading in the early 1980s and, as they were clearing the place, Adrian asked if he could take some of the postcards from the display rack that once hung outside the shop doorway.

At that time – the 1970s and 80s – Adrian was not a postcard-hunter, he was however an avid stamp-collector. Indeed, Adrian would still consider his philatelic activities his central focus, with postcards just a sideline or spin-off. Back then, he was acquiring postcards only in pursuit of stamps so that, for the most part, he acquired postcards by default, as it were – nevertheless, he acquired lots of them.

The postcards from the village shop sat in a box forgotten in a corner of his study and, along

with it, several other boxes of postcards that had accumulated as philatelic collateral detritus. Then, in the 1990s, married and moving into a new house – new *as a dwelling house*, that is, because it was his old village schoolhouse renovated and repurposed – Adrian's wife asked him to "do something" with his boxes upon boxes of "stuff".

So it was, for the first time, that Adrian got a few albums and laid out in an orderly fashion the postcards he wanted to keep. And it was from this his Cork postcard collection evolved.

IN THE SPRING or early summer of 2010 I'm walking down Main Street in Skibbereen one day and I meet Adrian Healy coming out of the post office, which is his place of work.

At that time I was doing a lot of writing for *The Southern Star* newspaper, feature-articles and the like. That particular day I was working on something for *StarLife*, a *Southern Star* magazine supplement – indeed, in my hand I had the final page-proof for what I was working on – a Michael Minihane photograph from 1967 of cockle-pickers on the strand at Crookhaven. *StarLife* had a regular feature on the last page called 'Final Frame' which took a photograph and with it put a little block of text telling the story behind the making of the picture.

I was always on the lookout for unusual images for this series. I knew Adrian was a great collector of stuff so I flagged up my interest in such items with him. In response, he told me about a picture he had of Raheen Castle in Myross – a 1930s postcard – with a 1930s motorcar parked in front of it. As a composition, he said, there was something intriguing about it. It sounded like just the kind of thing I was after – local but out of the ordinary (the card is reproduced on p. 81 of this book, top of the page).

By this way, shortly thereafter, I came to write a feature on Adrian Healy and his Cork postcard collection, a picture-rich version of which appeared in the pages of *The Southern Star*. Another version of it appeared in the *Irish Examiner* in August or September of that year.

Therefore, it must have been in the autumn of 2010 when Kinsale's John James got in contact with me to let me know that he too was a collector of Cork postcards. John James – who was someone I knew not at all – invited me, when next I was in Kinsale, to come up to his house and view the collection for myself, if interested.

Before going over to Kinsale I had presumed that the two collections would overlap considerably, but this was not so. In fact, the two collections *complemented* one another wonderfully: John James' collection is very strong on the east side of the county and weaker in parts of the far west, while Adrian's collection has exactly the opposite strengths and weaknesses. Both collections are sparse enough in areas of the northwest – however, places such as Newmarket and Knocknagree and Ballydesmond are not on established tourist trails – that is, cards for these places simply do not exist to the same extent as they do for, say, Rosscarbery or Ballycotton.

It was quite some time after that, however, before it occurred to me to do *a book* on the

The collectors: John James of Kinsale (left) and Adrian Healy of Skibbereen meet for the first time. Although both men had been collecting Cork postcards for decades – each building up a huge collection – they had never encountered one another until this meeting, which took place at Church Meadow House in Skibbereen in 2011. (Photo: Perry O'Donovan)

subject. I cannot remember exactly when the idea occurred to me – it must have been some time in 2011 (I was out hill-walking at the time) – but I remember the moment of inspiration. It was so *obvious* (as good ideas often are)! Had anyone done a book on the postcards of Cork before? I was not aware of such a book – but that did not mean too much because, having lived nearly half my adult life in Britain, there are lots of things of which I am not aware. However, the two collectors did not know of such a book either, which did mean something because these men had been collecting postcards for decades and would know if such a publication existed.

Web-searches confirmed the fact – a book on the postcards of Cork had never been done! Postcards of Galway, yes, Postcards of Limerick, yes, Postcards of Dublin, yes, even the Postcards of Cavan, but not Cork! (A number of publications have featured scatterings of Cork postcards, of course – especially city cards – but there has never been a dedicated and comprehensive production, covering the whole of the territory – city and county, from Allihies to Youghal and from Clonakilty to Charleville – deploying contemporary editorial treatment of the constituent elements.) And there was I with ready access to several thousand Cork postcards, all neatly laid out in albums, and – having spent the most of a decade working on volumes of the *Correspondence of Charles Darwin* at Cambridge University Library – just the right kind of editorial expertise to do the job, and do it well!

THE BOOK is presented in four sections: the city, west Cork, north Cork, and then, finally, east Cork, the idea being to make it something like a motoring tour – especially once one emerges from the city. The city itself is presented thematically – industry, transport, hotels, churches, etc. Then, eventually, via the river and Sunday's Well you come out to Ballincollig and begin to swing clockwise around the city and harbour, taking in the surrounding satellite towns – Blarney, Glanmire, Cobh, Carrigaline, and Crosshaven.

Then, by way of Kinsale, we head out into the west – Bandon, Clonakilty, Skibbereen, After Skibbereen we go out along the Mizen Peninsula to the very end and then come back in along the Beara Peninsula – Castletownbere, Glengariff, and Bantry.

Then, via Durrus and Drimoleague, to Dunmanway. And at Dunmanway we turn north into the north country – Inchigeela, Macroom, Millstreet and so on.

At Charleville, which is the end of the north Cork section, we head over to the other great northern-border stronghold of Mitchelstown, then down to Fermoy, and over to Youghal, and then, finally, coming through Midleton and Cloyne, we come back towards the city again. So that in the course of the book *we go twice around the city in a clockwise direction*, once touring the satellite territories surrounding city and the harbour area, and afterwards a second time, in a wider sweep, taking in the whole of the rest of the county.

In earlier drafts of this book I was doing very different kinds of captions, captions in which I would say what collection the postcard was from, who the publisher was (if it could be determined), and then where and when the card was posted – providing a detailed description of the stamp(s) and its post office cancellation mark(s) – and then, finally, provide a transcription of the message on the card, or of any printed notes. I did *not* get involved in discoursing on the subject of the picture at all – if it was Blarney Castle, for example, I did not say anything about the history or cultural significance of the place.

However, the end result was too much like a manuscript catalogue. To make the book a better reading experience, the decision was made to include short extracts from Cork's rich literary and cultural heritage – bite-sized tasters of Frank O'Connor, Elizabeth Bowen, William Trevor and the like.

Messages on postcards are necessarily brief and, usually, light-weight: "*Lovely weather. Hope you got the eggs. Jack's teeth are still giving trouble. See you on Sunday. Best wishes, Edith.*" So the extracts – being more considered compositions – give the book ballast and body, and grace. The rewritten (more reader-friendly) captions do that too to some extent but, nevertheless, the extracts have been retained because they make it so much more than a book about postcards.

A couple of final points: when I was working on the Darwin Correspondence Project we were encouraged to work with the awareness that we were writing for 'an Indonesian postgraduate'. It was a policy designed to help us counteract our natural Euro-centric tendencies – that is, not to write in a way that presumed that people know their way around London, or are familiar with the nuances of social hierarchy in this part of the world and so on. It is something I always try to do in whatever I'm writing, hence, in this book, readers are not expected to know that Stroud is in Gloucestershire or that Down is in Northern Ireland or that Éamon de Valera took part in the Easter Rising (or even what the 'Easter Rising' was, or when it was) – so all of these things are spelled out in full such that any educated person can follow what is going on (within reason) without having to go off and 'Google' stuff.

Also – a similar sort of thing – we do not expect that anyone will pick up this book and read it cover-to-cover. Someone from Buttevant, for example, may be interested only in the cards for Buttevant and its close surrounds and perhaps nothing else. Therefore, they may read only a handful of the captions, consequently captions are fully self-contained – that is, everything you need to know is there before you – there is no need to go scrambling off to appendices or anywhere else for supporting information.

Finally, I would like to take this opportunity to thank some of the people who have given many, many hours (and so much more) to the making of this book: Sean Dineen, Finn Adams, Sophie Pentek, Dominic Casey, Fintan O'Connell and all at Inspire, Michael Flaherty at the Charleville public library (see the Charleville cards on pp. 169-78) and, of course, the two collectors, John James and Adrian Healy, who in addition to everything else were kind enough to help with the final proof-reading of the cards.

Perry O'Donovan
Skibbereen, 2013

THE CITY

The City of Cork crest shows a ship with three masts in full sail on sea-water, the ship and sea seen between two towers, each topped with a flag, which ought to be St Patrick's saltire – a red X-shaped cross on a white field – with the wind carrying the flags in the *same* direction, not hither and thither as in this Ja-Ja "Heraldic Series" postcard from the John James collection. The motto beneath reads: 'Statio Bene Fide Carinis': a Safe Harbour for Ships. 'Ja-Ja' is a trademark registered in 1905 by Stoddart & Co., of Halifax in Yorkshire, England. This postcard was posted in Dublin in December 1907, to a Monsieur F. <<*name illegible*>>, 253 Chaussée de Malines, Anvers, Belgique. No message, just signed "7.12.05" and "Mary" on the picture side.

Above: A Valentine's Colourtone Series card from the Adrian Healy collection. This card was never posted. The green area pictured is in Gurranabraher which is northwest of the city centre.

This 'Killarney' ferryboat card from the John James collection appears to be a production of the City of Cork Steam Packet Company – there is no information on the reverse, it just says 'POST CARD'. The ship was built at the Pointhouse Shipyard of A. & J. Inglis of Glasgow – it was originally commissioned as 'Moorfowl' in 1915 by the Glasgow-based G. & J. Burns steam packet company, but delays because of the 1914-18 war resulted in the Burns company rejecting her in 1917 while the ship was still on the stocks. In 1919 she was completed as the 'Killarney' for the City of Cork Steam Packet Company. In 1920, however, G. & J. Burns finally did acquire the vessel, renaming it 'Moorfowl' as originally intended. This card was never posted.

Twin Screw s.s. "Killarney," 2,150 tons.
FISHGUARD AND CORK
Direct Express Passenger Service.
Thrice Weekly in each direction.
CITY OF CORK STEAM PACKET CO., LTD.

The Quays Cork.

A Lawrence card from the Adrian Healy collection showing the north channel of the River Lee flowing past Penrose Quay (on the right bank; the left bank is Merchant's Quay). This view is looking up-river towards St Patrick's Bridge, the reverse view of the middle card on p. 1. The card was posted in August 1906 to a Miss May Thompson, 26 Sailsbury Road, Cromer, England (Cromer is a seaside town in East Anglia): "Thanks very much for P.C.", the sender writes, "I am glad you are enjoying yourself. My teeth are bad yet. I expect you both will be well tanned when you come back. Julie."

CORK. SHANDON STEEPLE.

Built in the 1720s, the belfry of St Anne's Church, Shandon, is one of the emblems of Cork city. A peculiar feature of Shandon steeple is that the north and east sides are of red sandstone and the other two sides are of grey limestone. From the John James collection, this is a Raphael Tuck & Sons postcard, from their "Town and City" Series: Raphael Tuck & Sons, Raphael House, Moorfields, London, E.C. The card was never posted.

A National Museum of Ireland postcard from the John James collection. Late eighteenth century and early nineteenth century Cork glasswork is highly prized – work by Francis Richard Rowe or Daniel Foley, or from Thomas Burnett's Glass House Company on Hanover Street, or from the partnership of Philip Allen and Atwell Hayes on Patrick Street. This card was never posted.

Cork Cut Glass Salad Bowls   No. 28

GREETINGS FROM CORK

© John Hinde Ireland Ltd.

John Hinde cards from the Adrian Healy collection, neither of which has been posted. In the card above, which has Shandon steeple at its centre, photography is by D.P. Acevedo. To the left, the St Patrick Street card – or simply 'Patrick Street' as it is commonly known – photography is by P. O'Toole.

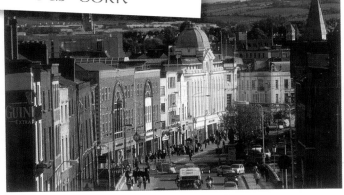

© John Hinde Ireland Ltd.

PATRICK STREET, CORK

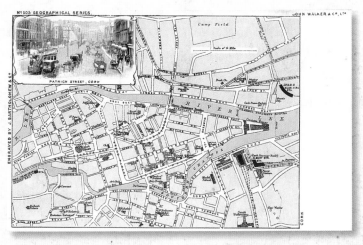

From the John James collection, this postcard is one of the 'Geographical Series' from Walker & Co., of Farringdon House, Warwick Lane, London. Each card in the Walker 'Geographical Series' consisted of a coloured map of an area with an inset photograph of a local feature, in this instance St Patrick's Street, the principal thoroughfare in Cork city. The maps were engraved by J. Bartholomew & Co.

A Fergus O'Connor card from the Adrian Healy collection sent to Master Jack Allen at the County Nursing Home, Regent Street, Coventry: "So glad you are getting on so well. Love from Auntie Kathleen." The monument in the picture is the Father Mathew statue at the top of St Patrick Street. Theobald Mathew (1790-1856), 'the Temperance Priest', was an anti-alcohol campaigner who founded the Cork Total Abstinence Society in 1838. The statue, by Irish sculptor John Henry Foley, dates from 1864.

A Lawrence postcard from the Adrian Healy collection showing St Patrick's Bridge, which crosses the north channel of the River Lee, and, in the foreground, Camden Place. This card was never posted.

From the Adrian Healy collection, a view of St Patrick's Street, looking north towards St Patrick's Bridge, published by Charles L. Reis & Co., of Dublin and Belfast. This postcard was never posted.

Cork City Hall postcard produced by Photocraft Limited, Dublin (John James collection). Cork City Hall (its Union Quay aspect is shown here) was built in the 1930s. This postcard was never posted.

The Metropole Hotel on MacCurtain Street, Cork, opened in 1897 (MacCurtain Street was then King Street). From its foundation it was an unlicensed premises (that is, it did not serve alcohol), and continued as such until the 1950s. From the John James collection, this postcard appears to be a hotel publication. The card was posted in 1913, to a Miss Doris Dove, at 16 Buller Street, Grimsby, Lincolnshire, England: "Dear Doris, a P.C. of the hotel where we are staying for your album. Cork is a beautiful place. Auntie Edyth."

From the John James collection, this view of Blackrock Castle is one of an "Oilette" series from the Raphael Tuck & Sons company. The Cork "Oilette" set, issued in 1909, had six cards: Blackrock Castle, Blarney Castle, Father Matthew's Quay, Queenstown Band Promenade, St Fin Barre's Cathedral, and St Patrick's Street. This postcard was never posted. On the reverse the following is printed: 'Blackrock Castle, which stands in a conspicuous position on the promontory of Rigmahon, is a modern turreted structure erected to provide a light for navigation purposes. It stands on the site of a seventeenth century castle of the Mountjoys and is supposed to be the spot from which William Penn embarked for America.'

" With deep affection and recollection
  I often think of the Shandon bells "—
Whose sounds so wild would, in days of childhood,
  Fling round my cradle their magic spells ;
On this I ponder, where'er I wander,
  And thus grow fonder, sweet Cork, of thee ;
    With thy bells of Shandon,
      That sound so grand on
The pleasant waters of the River Lee.

SHANDON CHURCH AND BELLS, ST. ANN'S, CORK.

THERE ARE certain things in all historic cities which tourists and no other people do. They are generally of a nature to confirm local inhabitants in the belief that all tourists are half-witted. In Cork you are supposed to kiss the Blarney Stone and to hear the Bells of Shandon.

When I arrived beneath the reddish steeple of Shandon Church, the bellringer was not in, and I became surrounded by an eager and obliging crowd of women wearing black shawls and by barefoot children, all deeply concerned in my affairs and all determined that I should hear the bells of Shandon without delay. Foremost among my assistants was a Mrs Driscoll, to whose tireless energy, I believe, in the end I owed the discovery of Mr Albert Wellington Meredith, the bellringer of Shandon – "the only Meredith in Cork, sir" – and the owner of a name both historical and political.

We went up into the belfry, where an octave of bell ropes hung down in the ringing gallery. Mr Albert Wellington Meredith braced himself for the effort, and, swaying his body backwards and forwards like the true virtuoso, shook from the steeple the sound of 'The Minstrel Boy'.

The bells of Shandon do, indeed, in the famous words of Fr Prout, 'sound so grand on the pleasant waters of the River Lee'. And Cork must know them by heart! Every time a curious visitor enters the belfry Mr Albert Wellington Meredith treats the city to a concert. He has been doing it for twenty-nine years, and he will tell you that in summer when Americans dash through Cork on their way to Killarney (which is all they see of Ireland!), the bells of Shandon are never silent all day long.

We had 'St Patrick's Day', 'The Harp that Once', 'Garryowen', and a wedding peal.

I looked through a window and saw that down below the barefoot children had gathered with financial expressions, glad that the tourist season had opened so hopefully.

Mr Albert Wellington Meredith then, from force of habit, offered to play me some American melodies, but I felt that Cork had probably had enough.

*From **In Search of Ireland** (1931), by H. V. Morton.*

Facing page: From the John James collection, the Shandon Church and Bells card is a 'Carbo Colour' postcard published by Valentine & Sons of Dundee and London. The postcard was never posted. The Church of St Anne Shandon, Church Street, Cork, built in 1720s, is one of the principal symbols of the city. A peculiar feature of Shandon steeple is that the north and east sides are of red sandstone and the other two sides are of grey limestone. First rung in 1752, St Anne's Shandon is celebrated for its ring of eight bells. The lines quoted on the card are the opening lines of 'The Bells of Shandon', by Francis Sylvester Mahony (1804-66), whose pen-name was 'Father Prout'. Cork-born Mahony was an Irish humorist and magazine editor; he began his career as a master of rhetoric at the Jesuit college of Clongowes Wood in Kildare; however, following expulsion from the order, he moved to London where he made his way by means of his pen. The lines printed are the lines of the opening stanza:

Shandon Cork.

With deep affection and recollection
I often think of the Shandon bells,
Whose sounds so wild would,
in days of childhood,
Fling round my cradle their magic spells.
On this I ponder, where'er I wander,
And thus grow fonder, sweet Cork, of thee,
With thy bells of Shandon,
That sound so grand on
The pleasant waters of the River Lee.

Above: This view of the steeple of St Anne's Shandon is an unposted American News Company card from the Adrian Healy collection.

Right: A Valentine card from the John James collection showing a King Street scene (now MacCurtain Street). This card was never posted.

King Street, Cork

From the Adrian Healy collection, this postcard of the courthouse on Washington Street was published by Fergus O'Connor. The card was posted in Ballincollig in December 1914, to a Mr F. Chatfield, of Smithfield Road, Uttoxeter, Staffordshire, England: "Compliments of the season to you, from Walter", it says, and "B'collig 23/12/14" is written as a footnote to the message. The main body of the courthouse dates from the 1890s, however the pillared front is from an older courthouse building – built in the 1830s – which burned down in 1891. In 1914 Washington Street would have been Great George Street (as in King George); it was renamed [George] Washington Street in 1918.

A postcard of the Cork School of Art building on what was then Nelson Place; today this is the Crawford Art Gallery and Café, and Nelson Place is Emmet Place. Further off, is the old Cork Opera House, which burned down in December 1955 (the present-day Cork Opera House was built in the 1960s, remodelled in the 1990s). This unposted card, from the John James collection, was published by E. R. Music Supply Stores, Cork.

School of Art and Opera House, Cork.

From the Adrian Healy collection, this view down the South Mall (looking west) is a 'Reliable Series' card from William Ritchie & Sons of London and Edinburgh. Posted in Fermoy in August 1908 to a Nurse Butts at 54 Noord Street, Johannesburg, South Africa: "Have had a letter from Bags", the message says, "Laps is gone to Roobrwood. Sent there by B – it is I believe the beginning of change. Goodness help me, Mac." The South Mall is the main commercial and legal district in the city. The building with the limestone columns was commissioned and constructed (in the mid-1800s) as the Cork Provincial Bank.

From the John James collection, an R.A. Series postcard featuring the Imperial Hotel on the South Mall (R. A. Series: Radermacher, Aldous & Co., Ludgate Hill, London). This card was never posted. Also featured on the card are representations of Blarney Castle, the Lakes of Killarney, and O'Sullivan's Cascade, which is also in the Killarney area.

View of the South Mall looking eastwards from Grand Parade, an unposted Valentine card from the Adrian Healy collection (Valentine & Sons, of Dundee and London). In the background (on the right side of the picture) can be seen the spire of Holy Trinity (also known as the Father Mathew Church) on Father Mathew Quay.

From the Adrian Healy collection, this Philco Publishing Company card offers a view (looking east) from St Patrick's Bridge: in the distance is New Bridge (now Brian Boru Bridge) traversing the north channel of the River Lee – the left bank is St Patrick's Quay and right is Merchant's Quay. This postcard was never posted.

From the John James collection, this view of St Patrick's Bridge from Merchant's Quay is a Fergus O'Connor card. The card was posted in April 1905, to a Miss Danmath, at 13 Albion Terrace, Alverthorpe Road, Wakefield, Yorkshire, England: "I don't think you have one of these", the writer says; "I will send you another next week. Awfully cold and wet up to noons." The message is unsigned.

This Dollard Tru-Colour Series postcard from the Adrian Healy collection shows Kennedy Quay (left), Horgan's Quay (right), and (centre of the picture) the meeting-point of Custom House Quay and Anderson's Quay. The card was posted in August 1960 to a Mr P. Ruane, at 1 Edward Street, Brighouse, Yorkshire, England: "Friday Eve", the message begins, "Got in at Moores [Hotel] about 4.00pm. No more sun since dinner. Tomorrow I am off for Bantry when I can find the road out. Hope you are both well", and is signed, "Billy."

In 1917, the Ford Corporation decided to establish a tractor-manufactory in Cork on the site of the old Cork Park Racecourse, near the Marina – Henry Ford had family connections with Cork. In 1919 the first 'Fordson' tractor built in Cork came off the production line. Later, in the 1930s, the Cork operation switched to car-manufacturing. About 1,800 people were employed at the plant in the inter-war years (which, in a country with a very small manufacturing sector, represented an important feature in the economic geography of the south of Ireland). Major extensions were made to the Marina Ford works after the Second World War, however, despite these, Ford manufacturing in Cork came to an end with the final closure of the factory in the early 1980s. The colour card is from the Adrian Healy collection. It is one of a Milton Post Card Series, never posted. The black and white card is from the John James collection and appears to be a Ford company production. Again this card was never posted.

Ford's Works, Cork.

HENRY FORD & SON LIMITED · CORK
THE LARGEST AUTOMOBILE PLANT IN IRELAND · ESTABLISHED 1917

Great Southern & Western Railway, Cork.

This unposted Philco Publishing Company card showing Cork Railway Station and part of Lower Glanmire Road is from the John James collection. The station was built by the Great Southern and Western Railway in the 1890s, amalgamating and replacing two older railway stations. Originally it was called the Glanmire Road Station, but was renamed the Kent Railway Station in 1966 in honour of Thomas Kent, a nationalist leader in the 'Easter Rising' of 1916.

A Royal Victoria Hotel card from the John James collection: the card is addressed to Mr <<*name illegible*>>, at 6 Carlisle Terrace, Kingstown, Co. Dublin, and dated 3 July 1903: "Dear Bea" it says, "I am rushing through & shall be home about 8 o'ck tomorrow evening. Ever yours, Lawrence." The Royal Victoria Hotel (the building with the flag in the picture above), situated at 35 and 36 St Patrick Street, 'the principal and most central street in Cork', offered a 'Reading Room, in which all the English, Scotch, Irish, and American Journals are filed, a News Room where American telegrams are received, 150 Bedrooms, 10 Suites of Apartments, a Drawing Room for Ladies, a Coffee and Commercial Room on the ground floor, two Billiard Rooms, a Smoking Room, Bath Rooms &c.' Also on this postcard, aside from a little representation of the Cork city crest, is an inset image of Blarney Castle. There is no publisher statement – it may be a Royal Victoria Hotel production.

From the Adrian Healy collection, a John Hinde composite card – (on the left side of the card) Cook Street with the spire of Holy Trinity in the background (top), English Food Market (middle), and (bottom) part of St Patrick Street; (on the right) South Gate Bridge by night with St Fin Barre's Cathedral in the background (top), Cook Street (middle), and County Hall. This card has never been posted.

GREETINGS FROM CORK

Right: A Valentine's postcard view of part of St Patrick Street (looking northwards to St Patrick's Bridge and St Patrick's Hill). This card, from the Adrian Healy collection, was never posted.

THE IMPERIAL HOTEL CORK

Left: This postcard picture of the Imperial Hotel on the South Mall is from the John James collection; the publisher is not identified (it may have been a hotel production); there is no other information on the reverse of this card (it just says 'POST CARD'), which was never posted.

TWICE A YEAR perhaps, on Saturday afternoons, there was going to Cork to the pictures. Clarke Gable and Myrna Loy in *Too Hot to Handle. Mr Deeds Goes to Town.* No experience in my whole childhood, and no memory, has remained as deeply etched as these escapes to the paradise that was Cork. Nothing was more lovely or more wondrous than Cork itself, with its magnificent array of cinemas: the Pavilion, the Savoy, the Palace, the Ritz, the Lee, and Hadji Bey's Turkish Delight factory. Tea in Thompson's or the Savoy, the waitresses with silver-plated tea-pots and buttered bread and cakes, and other people eating fried eggs with rashers and chipped potatoes at half-past four in the afternoon. The sheer sophistication of Thompson's or the Savoy could never be adequately conveyed to a friend in Skibbereen who had not had the good fortune to experience it. The Gentleman's lavatory in the Victoria Hotel had to be seen to be believed, the Munster Arcade left you gasping. For ever and for ever you could sit in the middle stalls of the Pavilion watching Claudette Colbert, or Spencer Tracy as a priest, and the earthquake in San Francisco. And for ever afterwards you could sit while a green-clad waitress carried the silver-plated tea-pot to you, with cakes and buttered bread. All around you was the clatter of life and of the city, and men of the world conversing, and girls' laughter tinkling. Happiness was everywhere.

From William Trevor's **Excursions in the Real World** *(Hutchinson, 1993).*

This postcard view of St Fin Barre's Cathedral from the John James collection is one of an "Oilette" series from the Raphael Tuck & Sons company (see the caption for the Blackrock Castle card on p. 5). This postcard was never posted. On the reverse of the card – aside from information about the Tuck company and the Oilette series – the following is printed: 'St Finn Barre's is a large and elaborate structure in the Transition Norman style built in 1865-80. It stands on the site of an earlier building founded by St Finn Barre in the seventh century, this structure after various vicissitudes being demolished in 1725, and followed by another building which in turn was destroyed to make room for the present cathedral.' St Finbarr (*fl.* 550-623), the first bishop of Cork, is the patron saint of Cork; the saint's name is variously spelled, 'Finn Barr', 'Fin Barre', 'Finbarr', 'Finbar', 'Fionnbarra', etc.

CORK. ST FINN BARRS CATHEDRAL.

Angel from S. Fin Barre's Cathedral.
E.W.Tristram.

From the John James collection, a picture postcard of one of a number of angels on the sanctuary ceiling of St Fin Barre's Cathedral, above the high altar at the east end of the building. This ceiling was executed in the 1930s by the artist and art historian Ernest William Tristram (1882-1952) working to the architect's original designs – William Burges (1827-81) was the architect of St Fin Barre's Cathedral. Posted on 24 August 1935, the message on the reverse reads: "Dear Sir, Many thanks for yours dated 22 Aug, few are so kind and thoughtful. I hope if you are here again you will let me know beforehand so that I may have the pleasure of meeting you. I write on this card as you may wish to have it. Again thanks. Yours Sincerely, L. Dobbin."

Eastern view,
St Finbarr's College, Farranferris, Cork

From the John James collection, postcards of St Finbarr's College, Farranferris, a seminary and secondary school attached to the Roman Catholic diocese of Cork and Ross. Established in 1887 the college finally went out of business in 2006. Farranferris is the *alma mater* of many well-known Corkonians, including the property developer Owen O'Callaghan, the television broadcaster Bill O'Herlihy, former Fianna Fáil cabinet minister Joe Walsh, and the composer Seán Ó'Riada. The school was renowned as a sporting college, particularly for GAA codes. These cards have not been posted, and offer no publisher information.

Front Entrance
St Finbarr's College, Farranferris, Cork

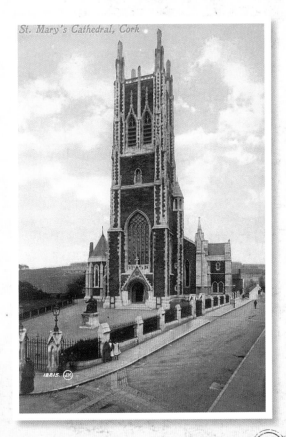

St. Mary's Cathedral, Cork

Right: The Cathedral of St Mary and St Anne, known locally as the North Cathedral, is situated at the top of Shandon Street, looking south over the city (it is known as the 'North Cathedral' to distinguish it from the cathedral on the south side of the city, which is the Church of Ireland's St Fin Barre's Cathedral). Dedicated in 1808, the Cathedral of St Mary and St Anne is the principal church of the Roman Catholic diocese of Cork and Ross. This Valentine's postcard from the Adrian Healy collection was never posted.

Opera House, Cork

THE REAL interest of Half Moon Street for me [was the] stage door of the Cork Opera House. This tall double door, arched and high-flung to give room for the scenery to enter and leave, was always open by day, venting stale air otherwise imprisoned for almost a hundred years, and that particular smell of all theatres… Frozen applause. The ghosts of words. Behind this arched door a wide stairway, iron-tipped, led up to the backstage area, generally closed off by a second double door guarded by old Downey, the stage-door keeper. In the summer it was often thrown open for ventilation, and then we small peepers on the pavement below could see hints of what was going on inside.

I would see men and women passing to and from the stage, hurriedly or slowly, a robed king with a crown, a pirate with a cutlass, ladies and gentlemen in rich clothes, beautiful girls in pink tights and tiny skirts, their arms, backs and bosoms paper-white, soldiers in red coats, armed cowboys, a Negro in chains, or a tattered beggar. It is not their strange costumes that I remember with passion but their Indian-coloured faces and red mouths, and their great eyes darkened and staring…

Every Sunday morning or Saturday night I would see at this arched door the departure, and every Sunday afternoon or Monday morning the arrival of forests, waterfalls, mountains, grey castles, panelled halls, mossy rocks, cannons, candlelabras, bundled swords and muskets, gold chairs, thrones, white clouds billowing up from or subsiding down on great drays drawn by hairy-legged draught horses. But who carried the golden throne, the grey castle, or the mossy rock out of the dusty gloom into the sunlight? It was Tommy Mulvaney or Jim Dooley who would then, darting across to the pub for a pint, pat me on the head and ask after my father. Who bore the blue skies, sagging like thirty-foot-long furled flags, up from the street to the stages' dim-lit maw? It was Lazy Casey or Georgie Cantwell, who might, tomorrow morning, be whitewashing the ceiling for my mother, or holding up the street corner by the quay waiting for the pub to open. There were no borders in my mind between this actuality and that fantasy. It seemed entirely natural to me when one day the doors were flung open (in the middle of a matinee of *A Royal Divorce*) to allow the acrid smoke of the Battle of Waterloo to creep out into Half Moon Street, and pouring out through its pungent clouds came the entire Napoleonic army, sometimes called the Cork Butter Exchange Band, clutching the instruments with which they had been playing the 'Marseillaise', dressed in Grand Army uniforms, hastening across to the Alaska Bar for foaming pints quaffed with rolling eyes and hearty moustache-sucking in the middle of the street. I was no more surprised the day I found Cinderella's white-and-gold coach standing in the cobbled yard of the cooperage…

From Sean O'Faolain's autobiography **Vive Moi** *(Rupert Hart-Davis, 1965).*

Facing page: View of the old Cork Opera House building, which burned down in December 1955 (the present-day Cork Opera House building dates from the 1960s, considerably re-modelled in the 1990s). This unposted card from the Adrian Healy collection was published by E. R. Music Supply Stores, Cork.

Cork. Shandon Steeple, St. Mary's Church and Priory from St. Patrick's Bridge.

A Fergus O'Connor card from the John James collection showing an electric tram coming over St Patrick's Bridge. This postcard was never posted. In the background the north channel of the River Lee flows between, on the left, Lavitt's Quay and, on the right, Camden Place and, further off on the right-hand bank, Pope's Quay. On Pope's Quay, St Mary's Church is the building with the six limestone columns.

The Quays Cork.

From the John James collection, this postcard view of Penrose Quay is a card by Lawrence Publishers, Dublin. This postcard was never posted. The reverse of the card is also print-stamped (in purple ink) with 'Wilkie & Son, Tourist Agents, Cork'. The building on the right of the picture with the four limestone columns was once the headquarters of the City of Cork Steamship Company.

This South Infirmary postcard, which is from the John James collection, does not have a publisher statement. The card was posted in March 1906 to C. J. Liebenberg Esq, P.O. Box 58, Klerksdorp, South Africa: "Are you smart in Euclid! If so prove the meaning of (four but five) <<name illegible>>"

C. W. Faulkner & Co., London, E.C.

"LEO," THE HOSPITAL DOG OF CORK.
(St. Bernard, Rough-coated).

The 'Leo the Hospital Dog of Cork' postcard is from the John James collection, published by C. W. Faulkner & Co., London. 'Leo' was a St Bernard dog that, in the 1890s and early 1900s, "collected" thousands of pounds for the Victoria Hospital in Cork. This postcard was posted in May 1906, to Miss Cooke, Bank Cottage, Great Bowden, Market Harborough, Leicestershire: "Dear S, Hope you are all well; if you don't write before Thursday write to us at The Laurels, Roehampton Park, Roehampton, SW. We are going there for 10 days or so. <<illegible>>as been in bed with a chill ever since she came home, so she did something for herself in going away. Love from <<name illegible>>"

This postcard of the Children's Ward at the Victoria Hospital is also from the John James collection. The card was published by The Scientific Press Ltd., London. Part of the money collected by 'Leo the Cork Hospital Dog' (see above) went towards the endowment of a cot in the children's ward at the Victoria, the 'Leo Cot.'

Children's Ward, Victoria Hospital, Cork.

This postcard of the South Presentation Convent is from the Adrian Healy collection. Published by the Photo Tourists' Association, Turnham Green, W. London, the card was posted in Cork in May 1905 to Sr M. St Canice at the Presentation Convent, Caherciveen, County Kerry: "My dearest Sister, You will be glad to see the old Convent I am sure. Sr Charles stands near the lady in white. The white novice is Sr Joseph – a new Sr Joseph & the sister in the distance is "yours truly." I had a letter from Dr Staunton in which he praises your schools very much & said how pleased he was to meet my pupil. Save from all – Sr M. Bona."

SOUTH PRESENTATION CONVENT, CORK.

This postcard of the River Lee at Sunday's Well at night with St Vincent's Roman Catholic Church on Sunday's Well Road in the background, is from the John James collection. The card was published by Valentine's, in their 'Moonlight Series', and posted in October 1906, to a Miss Read, at 64 Bicester Road, Aylesbury, Buckinghamshire, England: "dr J, so sorry I forgot your books, Yrs S<<*name illegible*>>."

This postcard of the Capuchin Monastery and College [St Francis College], Rochestown, Cork, is from the Adrian Healy collection. There is no publisher information (it may have been a fund-raising production by the college itself); the card was posted in Cork in November 1910, to a Miss Ellie Neville, Pallaskenry, Co. Limerick: "Thanks for your letter. Glad that all are well. This picture of my present surroundings may interest you. Give my best regards to all the friends. How is Pallas this cold weather? With gilt-edged regards, Seán Ó'Muirthile."

This postcard, showing the Lady's Well area of the city (in particular the Lady's Well Brewery of James J. Murphy & Co.), is part of the Adrian Healy collection. There is no publisher's statement. The card was posted in July 1905, to a Miss Barnes at 13 Goods Station Road, Tunbridge Wells, Kent, England: "Tuesday. I hope to come in by the 2 train on Friday & shall come up by bus. L.G."

This view of the Coal Quay Market, or 'Paddy's Market', was published by the Max Ettlinger company. This postcard, which is from the John James collection, was never posted.

The General Post Office in Cork, at the corner of Pembroke Street, to the left, and Georges Street (now Oliver Plunkett Street). This postcard, which is from the Adrian Healy collection, was never posted.

CORK.

STATIO BENE FIDA CARINIS

I ADMIRED my father... He had been a bandsman in the British Army, played the cornet extremely well, and had been a member of the Irishtown Brass and Reed Band from its foundation...

As he had great hopes of turning me into a musician too he frequently brought me with him to practices and the promenades. Irishtown was a very poor quarter of the city, a channel of mean houses between breweries and builders' yards with the terraced hillsides high above it on either side, and nothing but the white Restoration spire of Shandon breaking the skyline. You came to a little footbridge over the narrow stream; on one side of it was a red-brick chapel, and when we arrived there were usually some of the bandsmen sitting on the bridge, spitting back over their shoulders into the stream. The bandroom was over an undertaker's shop at the other side of the street. It was a long dark, barn-like erection overlooking the bridge and decorated with group photos of the band. At this hour of a Sunday morning it was always full of groans, squeaks and bumps.

Then at last came the moment I loved so much. Out in the sunlight, with the bridge filled with staring pedestrians, the band formed up. Dickie Ryan, the bandmaster's son, and myself took our places at either side of the big drummer, Joe Shinkwin. Joe peered over his big drum to right and left to see if all were in place and ready; he raised his right arm and gave the drum three solemn flakes: then, after the third thump the whole narrow

channel of the street filled with a roaring torrent of drums and brass, the mere physical impact of which hit me in the belly. Screaming girls in shawls tore along the pavements calling out to the bandsmen, but nothing shook the soldierly solemnity of the men with their eyes almost crossed on the music before them. I've heard Toscanini conduct Beethoven, but compared with Irishtown playing 'Marching through Georgia' on a Sunday morning it was only like Mozart in a girls' school. The mean little houses, quivering with the shock, gave it back to us: the terraced hillsides that shut out the sky gave it back to us; the interested faces of passers-by in their Sunday clothes from the pavements were like mirrors reflecting the glory of the music. When the band stopped and again you could hear the gapped sound of feet, and people running and chattering, it was like a parachute jump into commonplace.

*From 'The cornet-player who betrayed Ireland',
a short story in* **The cornet-player who
betrayed Ireland,** *a collection of Frank
O'Connor stories, selected and edited by Harriet
O'Donovan Sheehy and David Marcus (Poolbeg,
1981).*

Detail from a Hartmann postcard, see p. 22.

see p. 22.

THE MARDYKE, CORK

This Mardyke card is a Cardall postcard (Cardall Ltd, Dublin). The Mardyke (from the Dutch 'Meer Dyke', meaning sea-wall) is the south bank of the northern channel of the River Lee west of the city centre. This card, from the John James collection, has never been posted.

General View of Cork.

This is a Frederick Hartmann postcard from the Adrian Healy collection. It was never posted. The two church towers in the picture are St Anne's Shandon, on the left, and on the right, the North Cathedral (the Roman Catholic Cathedral of St Mary and St Anne). Frederick Hartmann is credited with convincing the post office authorities to accept postcards with divided backs, that is, with the address on one side and space for a message on the other – before this the whole of the back had to be given over to the address, otherwise the post office would not handle the card.

The 'Cork Jingle' postcard is a Frederick Hartmann card from the Adrian Healy collection – a 'jingle' is an Irish two-wheeled covered car. This card was posted in August 1907, to Joseph B. Kelly Esq., Ballyshrew, Downpatrick, [County] Down: "Many thanks for your P.C." it begins, which is evidently a summer holiday communication between two Blackrock College boys (Blackrock College in Dublin is one of the leading fee-paying schools in Ireland). "I'd have written long ago if I knew where you were. No word about going back yet. Charles going on Sat. Do not intend to go till Monday. Talk about popularity, I played two cricket matches since I came home one at Navan other at Athboy great weather since June until this week could not get your nose out. I suppose you visited B Rock. I don't believe Ryan and Jeoff are going to stay another in Rock. Very glad about F. Foy. I did not write to any at B.Rock but O'Connor so I am altogether ignorant about the things of College until I go back. You will probably be left there for another month. Will write when I return and tell you all the news." The closely-written message is signed "Patrick."

University College (Entrance) Cork.

A Lawrence postcard showing the UCC gatehouse (University College, Cork), from the Adrian Healy collection. The card was posted in Cork in September 1910, to H. R. Hewson Esq., "Keumore", Cumberland Park, Acton, London W: "Very many thanks for your letter of sympathy which was much appreciated. I expect your holiday is nearly over by this time. So I hope you had a very nice one, at any rate you've been fortunate in good weather. We've not had any rain this month until yesterday. I hope you fared as well. Hoping you are very well. Kind regards, yours A.K."

THEY DROVE in a jingle across Cork while it was still early morning and Stephen finished his sleep in a bedroom of the Victoria Hotel. The bright warm sunlight was streaming through the window and he could hear the din of traffic. His father was standing before the dressing-table, examining his hair and face and moustache with great care, craning his neck across the waterjug and drawing it back sideways to see the better…

Mr Dedalus had ordered drisheens for breakfast and during the meal he crossexamined the waiter for local news. For the most part they spoke at crosspurposes when a name was mentioned, the waiter having in mind the present holder and Mr Dedalus his father or perhaps his grandfather.

Well, I hope they haven't moved the Queen's College anyhow, said Mr Dedalus, for I want to show it to this youngster of mine.

Along the Mardyke the trees were in bloom. They entered the grounds of the college and were led by the garrulous porter across the quadrangle. But their progress across the gravel was brought to a halt after every dozen or so paces by some reply of the porter's.

Ah, do you tell me so? And is poor Pottlebelly dead?

Yes, sir. Dead, sir.

During these halts Stephen stood awkwardly behind the two men, weary of the subject and waiting restlessly for the slow march to begin again. By the time they had crossed the quadrangle his restlessness had risen to fever. He wondered how his father, whom he knew for a shrewd suspicious man, could be duped by the servile manners of the porter; and the lively southern speech which had entertained him all the morning now irritated his ears.

They passed into the anatomy theatre where Mr Dedalus, the porter aiding him, searched the desks for his initials. Stephen remained in the background, depressed more than ever by the darkness and silence of the theatre and by the air it wore of jaded and formal study. On the desk before him he read the word *Fœtus* cut several times in the dark stained wood. The sudden legend startled his blood: he seemed to feel the absent students of the college about him and to shrink from their company. A vision of their life, which his father's words had been powerless to evoke, sprang up before him out of the word cut in the desk. A broadshouldered student with a moustache was cutting in the letters with a jackknife, seriously. Other students stood or sat near him laughing at his handiwork. One jogged his elbow. The big student turned on him, frowning. He was dressed in loose grey clothes and had tan boots.

Stephen's name was called. He hurried down the steps of the theatre so as to be as far away from the vision as he could be and, peering closely at his father's initials, hid his flushed face.

But the word and the vision capered before his eyes as he walked back across the quadrangle and towards the college gate. It shocked him to find in the outer world a trace of what he had deemed till then a brutish and individual malady of his own mind. His recent monstrous reveries came thronging into his memory. They too had sprung up before him, suddenly and furiously, out of mere words. He had soon given in to them and allowed them to sweep across and abase his intellect, wondering always where they came from, from what den of monstrous images, leaving him always weak and humble and restless and sickened of himself when they had swept over him.

The leaves of the trees along the Mardyke were astir and whispering in the sunlight. A team of cricketers passed, agile young men in flannels and blazers, one of them carrying the long green wicketbag. In a quiet bystreet a German band of five players in faded uniforms and with battered brass instruments was playing to an audience of street arabs and leisurely messenger boys. A maid in a white cap and apron was watering a box of plants on a sill which shone like a slab of limestone in the warm glare. From another window open to the air came the sound of a piano, scale after scale rising into the treble.

Stephen walked on at his father's side, listening to stories he heard before, hearing again the names of the scattered and dead revellers who had been the companions of his father's youth…

– When you kick out for yourself, Stephen – as I dare say you will one of these days – remember, whatever you do, to mix with gentlemen. When I was a young fellow I tell you I enjoyed myself. I mixed with fine decent fellows. Everyone of us could do something. One fellow had a good voice, another fellow was a good actor, another

The University College card is from the Lawrence publishing house in Dublin. Before the university became University College, Cork – UCC – it was the Queen's College. This postcard, which was never posted, is from the John James collection.

could sing a good comic song, another was a good oarsman or a good racketplayer, another could tell a good story and so on. We kept the ball rolling anyhow and enjoyed ourselves and saw a bit of life and we were none the worse for it either. But we were all gentlemen, Stephen – at least I hope we were – and bloody good honest Irishmen too. That's the kind of fellows I want you to associate with, fellows of the right kidney. I'm talking to you as a friend, Stephen. I don't believe in playing the stern father. I don't believe a son should be afraid of his father. No, I treat you as your grandfather treated me when I was a young chap. We were more like brothers than father and son. I'll never forget the first day he caught me smoking. I was standing at the end of the South Terrace one day with some maneens like myself and sure we thought we were grand fellows because we had pipes stuck in the corners of our mouths. Suddenly the governor passed. He didn't say a word, or stop even. But the next day, Sunday, we were out for a walk together and when we were coming home he took out his cigar case and said: By the bye, Simon, I didn't know you smoked, or something like that. Of course I tried to carry it off as best I could. If you want a good smoke, he said, try one of these cigars. An American captain made me a present of them last night in Queenstown.

Stephen heard his father's voice break into a laugh which was almost a sob.

– He was the handsomest man in Cork at that time, by God he was! The women used to stand to look after him in the street.

He heard the sob passing loudly down his father's throat and opened his eyes with a nervous impulse. The sunlight breaking suddenly on his sight turned the sky and clouds into a fantastic world of sombre masses with lake-like spaces of dark rosy light. His very brain was sick and powerless. He could scarcely interpret the letters of the signboards of the shops. By his monstrous way of life he seemed to have put himself beyond the limits of reality. Nothing moved him or spoke to him from the real world unless he heard in it an echo of the infuriated cries within him. He could respond to no earthly or human appeal, dumb and insensible to the call of summer and gladness and companionship, wearied and dejected by his father's voice. He could scarcely recognise as his his own thoughts, and repeated slowly to himself:

– I am Stephen Dedalus, I am walking beside my father whose name is Simon Dedalus. We are in Cork, in Ireland. Cork is a city. Our room is in the Victoria Hotel. Victoria and Stephen and Simon. Simon and Stephen and Victoria. Names.

From *A Portrait of the Artist as a Young Man* (New York, 1916), by James Joyce.

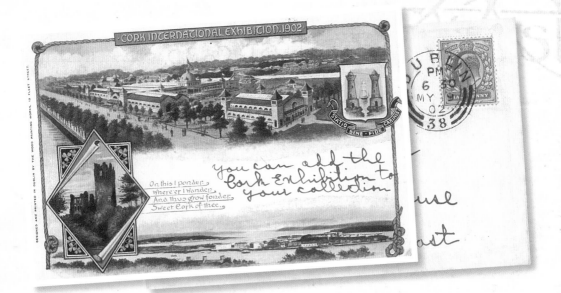

Cards commemorating the International Exhibition in Cork in 1902. A project of Edward Fitzgerald, the city mayor, the World's Fair type exhibition was staged in an eight hectare site on the west side of the city; the exhibition ran from the beginning of May to the end of October 1902. Afterwards the exhibition grounds became what is now Fitzgerald's Park, an urban parkland amenity. The card above is from the Adrian Healy collection. Designed and printed in Dublin by the Wood Printing Works, 13 Fleet Street, it was posted in

Dublin in May 1902 to a Miss A. McConnell at Strawmills House, Belfast. This was before the era of the 'divided back', so the reverse has the address only, with the message written on the front: "You can add the Cork Exhibition to your collection." The printed lines are from the opening stanza of Father Prout's 'The Bells of Shandon', see p. 7. The card below is from the John James collection. It was never posted and it has no printer or publisher statement.

View in Grounds.

CORK EXHIBITION, 1902

General Sir (Cornelius) Francis Clery (1838-1926) served in several British campaigns in Africa in the late nineteenth century – the Anglo-Zulu War in the 1870s, the campaigns in Egypt and Sudan in the 1880s, and the second Boer War. Clery was born at 2 Sidney Place, Wellington Road, Cork, the fourth son of James and Catherine Clery (née Walsh), Cork wine merchants. This postcard of General Clery, a Fergus O'Connor card from the John James collection, was never posted.

From the Adrian Healy collection, this Marina Walk card is one of B. & R.'s "Camera Series" (B. & R.: Brown & Rawcliffe of Liverpool). This postcard was never posted. Marina Walk runs along the south bank of the River Lee east of the city, near Ballintemple.

From the John James collection, the publisher of this Patrick Street card has not been identified. This postcard was never posted.

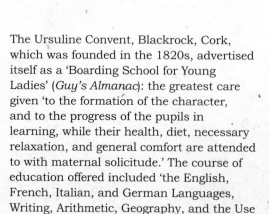

The Ursuline Convent, Blackrock, Cork, which was founded in the 1820s, advertised itself as a 'Boarding School for Young Ladies' (*Guy's Almanac*): the greatest care given 'to the formation of the character, and to the progress of the pupils in learning, while their health, diet, necessary relaxation, and general comfort are attended to with maternal solicitude.' The course of education offered included 'the English, French, Italian, and German Languages, Writing, Arithmetic, Geography, and the Use of the Globes; History, Sacred and Profane, Astronomy, Botany, Conchology, Mythology, the Practical and Popular Sciences, Architecture, and the elements of Geometry, Flower and Landscape Painting, and every description of useful and ornamental work.' These Lofthouse, Crosbie & Company postcards – from the John James collection – were never posted (Lofthouse, Crosbie & Co., of Tower House, Trinity Square, London, specialized in church and convent postcards).

The first concrete church in Ireland, Cork's Christ the King church at Turner's Cross was commissioned in the 1920s and opened on the Feast of Christ the King, 25 October 1931 (the architect was Barry Byrne, an American architect). The card with the photograph of the exterior of the church is from the Cardall company of Dublin. The artist's impression of the church is by John Wilson. The card with the photograph of the interior does not have a publisher statement. All three cards are from the John James collection. These postcards were never posted.

Christ King Church, Cork.

CHRIST THE KING CHURCH, CORK

SANCTUARY, CHRIST KING CHURCH, CORK.

This postcard view (looking west) of North Gate Bridge (now Griffith Bridge) is from the Adrian Healy collection, and was published by the American News Company. The card was never posted.

View at North Gate Bridge, Cork.

CORK — View from The Ferry Walk, Fitz-Gerald Park

This view of Sunday's Well (viewed from FitzGerald Park) is from the Adrian Healy collection. The address and addressee have been redacted, however the card was written by a P. Crowley and the stamp – a George V ½d adhesive stamp – was cancelled at Rosscarbery (the date on the cancellation mark is not clear): "Dear Briddie, How is Mam and Daddie and all my brothers and sisters. I hope they are all well. Well Briddie we are going home on Friday hoping you will come to meet us."

This Sunday's Well postcard is from the Adrian Healy collection, published by Fergus O'Connor. This card was never posted.

At the Ferry Sunday's Well, Cork.

From the Adrian Healy collection, a postcard showing a semi-rural Sunday's Well. The postcard has no publisher statement. On the reverse is written, "Dearest Alice, with loving wishes for a happy birthday. From Georgie", however – not stamped and stamp-cancelled – the card was not delivered by way of the post office.

ONE AFTERNOON after school I walked by myself all the way up to Sunday's Well which I now regarded as something like a second home. I stood for a while at the garden gate of the house where Mother had been working when she was proposed to by Mr Riordan, and then went and studied the shop itself. It had clearly seen better days, and the cartons and advertisements in the window were dusty and sagging. It wasn't like one of the big stores on Patrick Street, but at the same time, in size and fittings it was well above the level of a village shop. I regretted that Mr Riordan was dead because I would have liked to have seen him for myself instead of relying on Mother's impressions which seemed to me to be biased. Since he had, more or less, died of grief on Mother's account, I conceived of him as a really nice man; lent him the countenance and manner of an old gentleman who always spoke to me when he met me on the road, and felt I could have become really attached to him as a father. I could imagine it all: Mother

reading in the parlour while she waited for me to come home up Sunday's Well in a school cap and blazer, like the boys from the Grammar School, and with an expensive leather satchel instead of the old cloth school-bag I carried over my shoulder. I could see myself walking slowly and with a certain distinction, lingering at gateways and looking down at the river; and later I would go out to tea in one of the big houses with long gardens sloping down to the water, and maybe row a boat on the river along with a girl in a pink frock. I wondered only whether I would have any awareness of the National School boy with the cloth school-bag who jammed his head between the bars of a gate and thought of me. It was a queer, lonesome feeling that all but reduced me to tears.

'The Study of History', a story by Frank O'Connor, published in the short story collection **Domestic Relations** *(Hamish Hamilton, 1957).*

Two contemporary cards from the Adrian Healy collection (**top**) an Insight Ireland card showing St Patrick's Bridge and beyond it Bridge Street, and (**below**) a John Hinde postcard showing Cook Street, which runs at right angles off Patrick Street going towards the South Mall (in the background the spire of Holy Trinity church on Fr Mathew Quay can be seen). Neither card has been posted.

IRELAND CORK CITY

© John Hinde Ireland Ltd.

GREETINGS FROM CORK

From the John James collection, this army camp card was published by W. E. Mack of Hampstead (London). The following is written on the reverse: "Dear Auntie, just a line to say I arrived safe & sound after a 36 hours journey. The reason they called us back is, we are leaving here for Tidworth on Tues night, or Wed morning, instead of Friday night. Do not write back, I will let you know my new address as soon as possible. I am, Lovingly yours <<name illegible>> Remember me to all at Home. Goodnight." However, the card itself is not post-marked in any way so it may have been an enclosure in a letter, or possibly hand-delivered. The army barracks at Ballincollig was established in the early nineteenth century – between 1805 and

DON'T WORRY---I'm quite Comfortable at BALLINCOLLIG.

1815 – during the wars with Napoleonic France and its allies. Situated in 400 acres, the barracks housed garrisons during the First World War and during War of Independence.

View on the River Lee, near Cork.

Ballincollig is situated on the banks of the River Lee, a few miles west of Cork city. This Fergus O'Connor card, from the John James collection, was posted in Cork in 1905? to a Mr P. Dannatt, 13 Albion Terrace, Alverthorpe Road, Wakefield, Yorkshire, England (no message).

This mournful looking scene is a Fergus O'Connor postcard from the John James collection. The card was never posted,

On the road to Blarney.

BLARNEY CASTLE

From the Adrian Healy collection, a Real Ireland postcard of Blarney Castle, one of the iconic images of Ireland. Blarney is an old MacCarthy stronghold a few miles northwest of Cork city – a MacCarthy stronghold until the early 1700s after which it became the possession of the Jeffreyes family. The Blarney Stone itself is a block of bluestone built into the battlements of the castle and, according to lore, whoever kisses it is gifted with powers of eloquence and persuasiveness.The card was never posted.

CORK. BLARNEY CASTLE

From the John James collection, this postcard view of Blarney Castle is one of an "Oilette" series from the Raphael Tuck & Sons company (for more on Tuck's "Oilette" series on Cork, see pp. 5 and 14). This postcard was never posted. On the reverse of the card – aside from information about the Tuck company and the Oilette series – the following is printed: 'Blarney Castle, of which little now remains but the square donjon tower 120 feet high and a less substantial and lower ruin, was erected in the fifteenth century and was a stronghold of the McCarthys. The celebrated Blarney Stone, which is popularly supposed to impart persuasive powers to whoever shall kiss it, is found at the top of the tower in a somewhat awkward position below the parapet.'

This is a Lawrence card from the John James collection. Posted in Belfast in July 1904, addressed to Mrs J. Sanderson, 39 Barkers Road, Nether Edge, Sheffield, Yorkshire, England, the message reads: "If I miss my connection I will wire but expect to arrive home soon after 8 o/c " On the front is printed:

GOIN' TO KISS THE RA'AL BLARNEY
STONE
With quare sinsashuns and palpitashuns,
A kiss I'll venture here, Mavrone,
'Tis swater Blarney, good Father Mahony,
Kissin' the Girls than that dirty stone.

GOIN' TO KISS THE RA'AL 'BLARNEY STONE.
With quare sinsashuns and palpitashuns,
A kiss I'll venture here, Mavrone,
'Tis swater Blarney, good Father Mahony,
Kissin' the Girls than that dirty stone.

Street in the Village of Blarney.

This Blarney postcard, from the Adrian Healy collection, was never posted. This card has no publisher statement

St. Ann's Hydro (East View).

Modelled on James Wilson and James Manby Gully's very successful hydrotherapy establishment at Malvern, Dr Richard Barter (1802-70) opened a hydrotherapy establishment on St Ann's Hill near Blarney in the 1840s. *Guy's Postal Directory of Cork* for 1886 advertised the St Ann's Hill Hydrotherapy Establishment as having a circulating library, a reading room, covered tennis courts, three grass tennis courts, a theatre, an American bowling alley, and a billiard room for both ladies and gentlemen. St Ann's promoted itself as a residence for invalids and also offered health spa accommodation for tourists visiting the area. Barter went on to become the owner of (or at least closely associated with) several other establishments throughout Ireland, however none as successful as St Ann's. Dr Barter died in 1870, but members of the Barter family continued operating St Ann's until 1952. This card (which is from the John James collection) was never posted. It was published by J.J. O'Leary, Tram House, St Ann's Hill, Cork.

THE DINING ROOM, ST. ANN'S HILL HYDRO.

From the John James collection, a postcard showing the dining room at St Ann's Hill Hydro. This card was published by the proprietors of St Ann's. It was never posted.

PLACE POSTAGE STAMP HERE.

How do you Like this card my Sweet. How I wish You were Here How happy we should be.

Published by Hely's of Dublin this card is from the John James collection. It has no address nor is it postmarked in any way, however on the reverse is written, "My darling, How do you like this card my Sweet. How I wish you were here. How happy we should be." On the picture side is written: "This is a room in Hydro, of course not our room."

This picture of St Mary's and All Saints Church of Ireland, Glanmire, from the John James collection, is an 'Emerald Series' card. The Emerald Series cards were produced by the Irish Pictorial Post Card Company, operating out of 9 and 10 Maylor Street and Eagle Works, South Mall, Cork. This postcard was never posted.

FOTA HOUSE
Fota Island, Carrigtwohill
County Cork, Ireland
Telephone 021 812555

This Fota House postcard, which is from the John James collection, offers no publisher information and was never posted. Fota House was originally a modest hunting lodge belonging to the Smith-Barry family. The family lived in Britain, coming to Ireland for fishing, shooting, hunting, and yachting. In the 1820s, John Smith-Barry (1793-1837) decided to make Fota his full-time home and had the place rebuilt as a Regency-style country house. "Boutez-en-Avant" is the medieval war cry of the de Barry family, roughly translating as "Kick your way through." The de Barry family is of Welsh-Norman origin which once held extensive land holdings in Wales (in Pembrokeshire) and in South Munster, particularly in County Cork – the name of the town of Buttevant, for example, is supposed to derive from the "Boutez-en-Avant" war cry. Since the death of the last of the Smith-Barrys in 1975, the estate – comprising of 47 hectares of parkland including gardens and an arboretum, all of which is on Fota Island on the eastern side of Cork Harbour – passed through various wardships, including that of University College Cork and the Fota Trust. The Irish Heritage Trust took over responsibility in 2007.

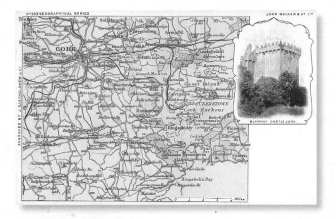

A John Walker card from the John James collection, part of John Walker's 'Geographical Series' (map engraved by J. Bartholomew & Co.): John Walker & Company, Farringdon House, Warwick Lane, London. This postcard was never posted.

The Silverspring Starch Company in Glanmire was established in 1870s. This card, which is from the John James collection, appears to be a company production. The card was never posted. Starch is a carbohydrate consisting of a large number of glucose units; it is produced by all green plants as an energy store. It is the most common carbohydrate in the human diet and is contained in large amounts in staple foods such as potatoes, wheat, maize, and rice. Pure starch is a white, tasteless and odourless powder that is insoluble in cold water or alcohol. It is processed to produce many of the sugars in processed foods. Dissolving starch in warm water gives a wheat-paste, which can be used

as a thickening, stiffening or gluing agent. The biggest industrial non-food use of starch is as an adhesive in paper-making. The word 'starch' is derived from the Middle English 'sterchen', meaning to stiffen.

This Frederick Hartmann picture postcard of the Holy Well at Aghada, which is from the John James collection, was posted in Newcastle, county Down, in July 1906, to a Miss Carey of 36 Gubyon Avenue, Herne Hill, London. (Aghada is on the east side of Cork Harbour.) The message reads: "This is the first stage of our tour. We are having most glorious weather. Will write very soon. Mother is sending you some eggs. No time for more, Yours Tony."

Trabolgan, Whitegate, Co. Cork.

Trabolgan House and its 1,500 acre estate, which is on the eastern side of the mouth of Cork Harbour, near Roche's Point, was owned by the Roche family up until the early 1900s. The Irish Land Commission purchased the estate and during the Second World War it was used as a base by a unit of the Irish Army. In the 1950s it was developed as a Pontin's Family Holiday Park. Trabolgan is still a leisure centre enterprise (Trabolgan Holiday Village) but it has been through several ownership regimes and redevelopments since the 1960s. This card, which is from the John James collection, is a production of Irish Luxury Holidays Limited ('Photogravure Printing by Hely's Limited'). The card was never posted.

Staff Sergeants & Sergts. 49 Co. R.G.A.

On the back of this card, which is from the John James collection, is written "Spike Island, August 1906." The card was never posted and there is no publisher statement. Spike Island is an island of 103 acres in Cork Harbour. It was purchased by the British government in 1779, becoming the site of Fort Westmoreland, housing the British authorities' arsenal in the south of Ireland. From the 1840s the place was used as a prison camp and convict depot, warehousing convicts prior to penal transportation to Australia. During the Irish War of Independence IRA prisoners were held there. Following the Anglo-Irish Treaty, the island remained as one of the so-called 'Treaty Ports', and was not handed back to the Free State until 1938.

The Rob Roy Hotel, Queenstown.   James O'Connor, Proprietor.

Rob Roy Hotel, West Beach, Queenstown [Cobh], Cork. Cobh is the principal town on Great Island in Cork Harbour. In 1849 what was then 'The Cove of Cork' was renamed 'Queenstown' in honour of the visit of Queen Victoria (see p. 45). In the 1920s, following the establishment of the Irish Free State, the town was renamed 'Cobh', which is a Gaelicized form of 'Cove'. This card was published as part of the "Emerald Series" from the Irish Pictorial Post Card Company in Cork. The card is from the John James collection and was never posted.

Published by the American News Company of New York, Leipzig, and London, this card from the John James collection looks southwest over Cork Harbour, showing in the foreground part of the Queenstown [Cobh] railway station and in the distance Haulbowline Island (a naval base – a British naval base then, still is for the Irish Navy). This postcard was never posted.

Queenstown Harbour and Railway Station.

This card, which is from the John James collection, appears to be a Cunard Line production (on the reverse is printed the company's contact details). The postcard was never posted. The Cunard Line – for generations the market leader in transatlantic passenger transport – was founded in the 1840s by Samuel Cunard. Being the first (or last) port of call in Europe, in the golden age of transatlantic liner traffic (1840s to 1940s), Queenstown/Cobh was a place of considerable economic and cultural significance – hotels, shipyards, a naval base, a multitude of catering service companies, financial and communication facilities, etc, etc; it was also home to two yacht clubs – the Royal Cork and the Royal Western – and even a cathedral – St Colman's Cathedral is the seat of the Roman Catholic diocese of Cloyne.

CUNARDER AT QUEENSTOWN

Right: A Real Ireland card showing Cobh waterfront with St Colman's Cathedral in the background. This card, from the Adrian Healy collection, has never been posted. The neo-Gothic St Colman's, by the architects Edward Welby Pugin (1834-75) and, subsequently, George Coppinger Ashlin (1837-1921), is nineteenth century – begun in 1868 but not finally completed until the 1900s. St Colman's Cathedral is the seat of the Roman Catholic diocese of Cloyne.

COBH

IRELAND

Below: From the John James collection, a Mason's "Aero" Series card (photo by Aerofilms Limited of London). This card has never been posted.

Aerofilms   COBH (QUEENSTOWN) CO. CORK.   42339.

Facing page: From the Adrian Healy collection, an Avon Sales card (Plastichrome, by COLOURPICTURES PUBLISHERS, INC, Boston 30, Mass. U.S.A.) showing the waterfront at Cobh with St Colman's Cathedral in the background. This postcard was never posted.

COBH IS ONE of the most attractive towns in Ireland. It is built on a steep hill above the harbour, with two jolly squares facing the sea, and is all jumbled and cluttered, and full of pubs and ironmongers. A few big ships come and go, there is a constant movement of small boats across the harbour, and high above it all St Colman's still stands in grey protection. But when I went up there one day to think about the place, looking out across the wide bay and its islands (one a well-known penal settlement, one the main base for the half a dozen ships of the Irish Navy), a sense of heartbreak overcame me all the same. The harbour which had looked so bright and bustling when I walked up the hill, now seemed desolate. The islands lay there loveless. Through the headlands the open sea looked cold, unwelcoming and unending, as though it had no farther shore; and the great church behind my back suddenly seemed to me the image of valediction, forever waving goodbye, regretfully and perhaps reproachfully, to the ships we could no longer see.

I very soon, however, cheered up, when I walked down West View again, it being a street of brightly painted gabled houses jammed together on so precipitous a slope that they looked as though they might at any moment slither all the way down to the sea. West View is enough to cheer up a manic depressive, and in my experience, Ireland itself is just the same. If a passing cloud, or a hangdog hamlet, an item of news from Crossmaglen, a historical memory or a ruined house can plunge one instantly into melancholy, just as abruptly cheerfulness breaks in. Like the clown of tradition, Ireland is a mixture of merriment and pathos…

*From **Ireland: your only place,** by Jan Morris (Aurum Press Limited, 1990).*

A Valentine card from the Adrian Healy collection showing the old clubhouse of the Royal Cork Yacht Club. The Royal Cork is believed to be the oldest sailing club in the world – in the 1720s William O'Brien, the 9th Lord Inchiquin, and several of his friends got together to formalise their sailing (and dining) activities and in so doing established 'The Water Club of the Harbour of Cork', which in the following century evolved into the Royal Cork Yacht Club. Originally the clubhouse was Inchiquin's castle on Haulbowline Island, however, during the wars with Revolutionary France the British Navy took possession of Haulbowline, and the club relocated to

ROYAL YACHT CLUB HOUSE, QUEENSTOWN

the Cove of Cork (present day Cobh). In the 1960s the club relocated again, to Crosshaven, just west of Cork Harbour. This postcard was never posted.

A Valentine card from the Adrian Healy collection. This patriotic card was produced during the First World War (1914-18). The men featured are, on the left, King George V and Lord Kitchener, and on the other side Admiral Sir John P. Jellicoe and Field Marshal Sir John French. The flags are, on the left, the British Union flag and the tricolour of the French Republic, and, on the right, the Russian naval ensign for the Imperial Russian fleet and the tricolour of Belgium (in defence of whose integrity and sovereignty Britain had gone to war in August 1914). The card proclaims (at the top) 'We are keeping the flag flying at Queenstown' (and at the bottom) 'We are doing our duty with a hearty good-will for the Empire, the Flag, and the Right.' The card was never posted.

WE'RE KEEPING THE FLAG FLYING AT QUEENSTOWN

Queenstown Harbour.

We are doing our Duty with a hearty Goodwill.
For the Empire, our Flag, and the Right.

Facing page: A Fergus O'Connor card from the John James collection, posted in Cork city in 1907 to Mr J. Cuddiford, Ambarrow Hill, Sandhurst, Camberly, Berkshire, England: "Dear Jack and Nell, We arrived quite safe after a rough trip. Hope you are all well & you got your Basket alright. Mags our address: Military Foot Police, Cork Barracks, Ireland."

August 2 [1849]
on board the "Victoria & Albert"
in the Cove of Cork, Ireland

Arrived here after a quick, but not very pleasant passage… close to the Cove of Cork many bonfires could be seen on the tops of the hills, and rockets sent off & lights burnt from different steamers. The entrance to the immense Harbour is very fine, though the land surrounding it is not very high. The effect of entering the Harbour by twilight was beautiful…

August 3 [1849]
on board the "Victoria & Albert"
The Cove of Cork

We woke at ½ p. 7, after a very good night's rest. The day was grey and excessively muggy which is characteristic of the Irish climate. . . . The ships saluted at 8 – the "Ganges" (the Flag Ship) & the "Hague", both 3 deckers, but the latter cut down, with a screw and many heavy guns put into her. Being very close to us, they made a great noise. The Harbour is very extensive, & there are several islands in it, one of which, Spike Island, is very large & has a prison in which convicts are confined; near it is another, with the depots &c.

In a line with this is the town of Cove, picturesquely built, up the side of a hill.

The 2 war ships only just came in & the Admiral (Dickson) & the Captain of the vessels came on board. Later, Lord Bandon (L. Lieut. of the County), L. Thomond, & Gen. Turner, Commander of the Forces at Cork, also came to pay their respects.

Albert went on shore, & I occupied myself in writing & sketching. He returning for luncheon which was earlier & at 2, with the Ladies & Gentlemen we embarked on the "Fairy", which was surrounded with rowing and sailing boats. We 1st went round the Harbour, all the ships saluting, as well as numbers of steamers and yachts & then went to Cove where we lay alongside the landing place, which was covered with people & very prettily decorated. Yachts and boats were crowding all around. The 2 Members, the Governors Roche & Power, as well as other gentlemen, including Roman Catholic and Protestant Clergy, presented an Address, followed by the members of the Yacht Club, after which to give satisfaction to the people, the place was called Queen's Town in honour of being the 1st place on which I had set foot on Irish soil. We stepped on shore amidst the near roar [of] cannon (the Artillery having been placed so close as quite to shake the handsome room we entered) & the enthusiastic shouts of the people.

Queen Victoria's Journals
(Vol. 27, pp. 270-3)
Royal Archives, Windsor Castle,
Windsor, Berkshire, England

Two views of West Beach on Main Street, Cobh: the coloured card is a Valentine's card from the Adrian Healy collection. This postcard has not been stamped or post-marked in any way but on the reverse the following is written "Near Railway Station, on right side of juncture – shop where I got the portrait (pencil)."

A Cardall picture postcard (Cardall Ltd, Dublin) from the Adrian Healy collection. This postcard was never posted.

"Reliable Series" postcard from the John James collection showing St Mary's, the Anglican church in Queenstown/Cobh ("Reliable Series" is a series published by William Ritchie & Sons Ltd of Edinburgh and London). This postcard was never posted.

A Fergus O'Connor card from the John James collection posted to a Master F. V. Faulkner, at Mounsey Road, Tranmere, Birkenhead, Cheshire England: "Dear Frankie", the message begins, "Many Happy returns of the day. Would you like to go for another sail. Dad."

Tender with American Mails, Queenstown Harbour.

A Cynicus card from the John James collection. This card was never posted. The Cynicus Publishing Company was based in Tayport in Fife, Scotland; 'Cynicus' was the pseudonym of Glasgow cartoonist Martin Anderson (1845-1932). Cynicus cards were often packed with figures like this one, with the name of the local town or seaside resort overprinted on the basic card. "Last Train to [wherever]" was another standard Cynicus production.

OUR LOCAL EXPRESS Queenstown to Cork

A Valentine card from the Adrian Healy collection showing a view of Whitepoint, which is at the west end of Queenstown/Cobh. Posted in Cork in October 1911 to a Miss Hambling, 33 St John's, Worcester, England: "We shall be coming home next Saturday all being well, F. Wilson."

Whitepoint, Queenstown

From the John James collection, this Monkstown Castle card does not have a publisher statement, however it records that the photograph is by J. H. Audley of Passage West, Co. Cork. The card was posted in Cork in 1962 to a Miss Malone of Termon, Barnhill Road, Dalkey, Dublin; the message reads: "This is quite near. A fine old place. Weather awful most of the time. The worst they have had all summer.

I'll be home about Friday. Saw *Mauretania* in last night but the mist spoiled the view. Dixon." The *Mauretania* was a Cunard company ocean liner operating between Southampton and New York. Dating from the mid-seventeenth century, Monkstown Castle, a fortified house on the western side of Cork harbour, looks out over the seaway leading up to Lough Mahon and Cork city.

This Emerald Series card from the John James collection was posted in Norwood, South East London, in 1907, to a Master R. Phillips, at 109 Gassiott Road, Tooting, South West London: "D. R., just a line to wish you very many happy returns of the day. Please tell your mother that if fine we

shall be please[d] to come over to see you all. With love & all best wishes, from your affectionate Auntie." Emerald Series cards were produced by the Irish Pictorial Post Card Company, operating out of 9 and 10 Maylor Street and Eagle Works, South Mall, Cork.

This Lawrence card showing the view from Great Island in Cork Harbour looking over to Monkstown (across the seaway leading up to Lough Mahon and Cork city) is from the Adrian Healy collection. The card was posted in Cork in 1908 to a Master Samuel Farmer, at 179 Fishpool Street, St Albans, Hertfordshire, England: "With Teacher's Love" is all the message says.

A card from the John James collection. There is no publisher statement for this card. The card was posted in Queenstown [Cobh] in October 1904, sent to a Miss Croley, Hibernia Buildings, Cork: "Did you ever cross the ferry here. HBC."

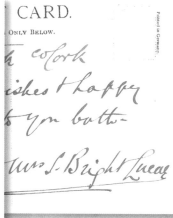

This Lawrence card showing the view from Great Island in Cork Harbour looking over at Glenbrook and Passage (across the seaway leading up to Lough Mahon and Cork city) is from the Adrian Healy collection. Although it is not stamped or post-marked in any way, the card was dispatched and delivered by some means because it was used as a New Year's greeting card: "With best wishes & happy new year to you both", the greeting goes, and it is signed "Mr & Mrs S. Bright Lucas", with the address "Dunedin Lodge, Glenbrook, Co. Cork." On the picture side of the card there is an arrow pointing to a house on the Glenbrook side of the seaway, presumably Dunedin Lodge.

Main Street, Carrigaline.   Co. Cork.

This Lawrence card showing Main Street, Carrigaline, is from the John James collection. The card was never posted. Carrigaline is a village 14 kilometres south of Cork city – at least, it was a village when this card was published: according to the 1901 census returns there were less than 500 people living there (476 persons in 1901, and 518 in 1911). The 2011 census recorded 14,775 people living in Carrigaline.

A Lawrence card from the Adrian Healy collection. This postcard was never posted. The village of Crosshaven is on the southern bank of the Owenboy River estuary, where the river meets the waters of Cork Harbour.

Carrigaline Road, Crosshaven, Co. Cork.

Crosshaven Co. Cork.

This postcard from the Adrian Healy collection was published by the Lawrence Company. The card was never posted. Crosshaven was the end of the line for the Cork, Blackrock, and Passage railway service. The extension southwards from Passage to Carrigaline and Crosshaven opened in 1904. The railway closed in 1932.

This Valentine card of Crosshaven from the Adrian Healy collection was never posted. The village of Crosshaven is on the southern bank of the Owenboy River estuary, just at the mouth of the estuary where it meets the waters of Cork Harbour.

This American News Company card from the John James collection was never posted. For other American News Company cards, see, for example, the Queenstown/Cobh railway station card on p. 41, and their Shandon church steeple card on p. 7.

This Lawrence card of a Crosshaven street scene from the John James collection was never posted.

This postcard, which was never posted, is from the John James collection. It is one of an "Oilette" series from the Raphael Tuck & Sons company (Raphael Tuck & Sons, Raphael House, Moorfields, London). Tuck's Cork, Bandon and South Coast Railway, "Sunnyside of Ireland", set were issued in 1905, this card is one of three in the set – the other two being 'Bantry Bay, where the French landed in 1798' and 'Glengarriff Harbour'. For other Cork-related Tuck cards, see the cards from the 'Town and City' series, p. 2, and the Cork set, pp. 5, 14, and 35.

This John Hinde card showing the old terminal building at Cork Airport is from the Adrian Healy collection. On the back of the card the following information about Cork airport is recorded: 'Cork Airport was opened in October 1961 and established direct connections with the South of Ireland and Dublin, Western England, London, and the Continent. It stands on 500 acres with two runways, the larger measuring 6,000 feet capable of handling jets, and the other 4,300 feet. The 80 ft high control tower dominates the airport. In it is housed every modern electronic aid for aviation.' This card was posted in Cork in August 1980, to Mrs D. Harwood, 22 Cherry Orchard, Marlborough, Wiltshire, England: "Travel not too bad. Trains very good but had long delay at Pembroke Docks. 9½ hours seems a long time on Ship. We have awful weather cant get to places. Hope you are having a nice holiday. Peggy must be in over now, not good weather down there at any time. The place is full of visitors now from Dublin Horse Show. What a time they had with rain. The wind is blowing outside (Ballybunion – laugh). Love to you and Don."

© John Hinde Ireland Ltd.

The Terminal Building, Cork Airport, Ireland.

Photo : E. Nägele, John Hinde Studios.

INTO THE WEST

© John Hinde Irreland Ltd.

KINSALE

Two contemporary postcards showing Kinsale as a prosperous tourist town: (**above**) a John Hinde card showing part of the harbour and the town centre (Acton's Hotel and Pier Road are on the left of the picture); and (**below**) a Real Ireland card of a street scene in the town centre (the corner of Market Lane and Market Square with the belfry of St Multose Church showing in the background). Both these postcards are from the Adrian Healy collection, neither of which has been posted.

KINSALE

MARKET STREET, KINSALE

From the Adrian Healy collection, a Fergus O'Connor postcard of a Market Street scene in Kinsale. There is no address or stamp on this postcard, however, on the reverse someone has written "You go up or down this street, turn around a corner, up another street, and you have been to Kinsale."

ST. MULTOSE, CHURCH OF IRELAND, KINSALE.

From the John James collection, this St Multose card is a Real Photo Production postcard. This postcard was never posted. Parts of St Multose church date from Norman times – that is, the 12th and 13th centuries. The church was built on the site of an even older religious foundation, a monastery founded by St Multose in the 6th century.

A Fergus O'Connor card from the John James collection showing the same view as the John Hinde card on the p. 53. This card was never posted; on the reverse "7/8/16" is written in pencil.

General View of Kinsale from James Fort

Below: The Hooded Cloaks card is an Insight Ireland card, also from the John James collection, and again not post-marked or written upon in any way. There is nothing especially that identifies this card as a Kinsale card; it is simply that John James has it with his Kinsale cards, perhaps because these cloaks are oftentimes called 'Kinsale cloaks.'

Traditional Hooded Cloaks as worn by the women of West Cork, Ireland.

Below left: From the John James collection, a Milton Series postcard from the Woolstone Bros. firm, of Milton Street, London. This card has never been posted

Below right: An Insight Ireland card from the Adrian Healy collection showing a little of Summercove (the church on the hill in the background is St Catherine's). This card has never been posted.

The Old Head of Kinsale card is from the Adrian Healy collection. It is a Fergus O'Connor postcard posted in January 1909, to M. O'Regan, Model School, Trim, Co. Meath: "I hope yourself and Mrs O'R & children are all well. Very kind of you to send card. I have no time for courtesies of that kind this year. Overwhelmed with Old Age Pension work all winter. Working usually till 3AM & often to 4AM & I cannot see the end yet. Sundays & Christmas Day the same as other days. Our Pension Officer here in the south has gone to Lunatic Asylum. Surprising many more have not gone there. How is Tim going on? How do you like Paddy's novel in the "Chronicle"? Diarmuid Ua <<*illegible*>>."

The [British] Old Age Pensions Act of 1908 introduced the old age pension from 1 January 1909, paying a non-contributory amount of between one and five shillings a week for persons aged 70 and over on a means-tested basis – to qualify recipients had to have an income of less than £21.10s. per year. Recipients also had to pass a 'character test', only those with a 'good character' could receive the pensions – that is, no drunkards, criminals, 'lunatics', or those considered habitually work-shy, etc. Despite the many restrictions and caveats, over 170,000 people in Ireland qualified for the benefit, one of the foundation stones of the modern welfare state.

Right: An Insight Ireland card from the Adrian Healy collection (photography by Peter Zöller). This card has not been posted.

KINSALE

Kinsale Harbour

Left: A postcard from the John James collection. There is no publisher statement on this card. It was posted in France to a Monsieur Louis Jansen, Rue Guilleminot 5, Dunkerque, with the message: "Bonne Santé, G. Jansen."

JACKDAWS nest in the limes of Friary hill, tear twigs, lay eggs, raise young, drop eggshells and whiten with their squirted lime-shit the newly washed limousines lined up for Mass, strut about on the road. A robin calls "Swing low, sweet chariot!" over by the French Prison and from near the slaughterhouse on Chairman's Lane a blackbird answers "Aujourd'hui! Aujourd'hui!" as the legless man is pushed in his wheelchair into a waiting car, and the Buck goes bounding down the narrow stairs and out into the freshness of Cork Street, jacket hooked over one finger, humming "The Mountains of Mourne", released from arranging that evergreen lament for his male voice choir.

Daybreak comes early in June to the port, with a bantam cock crowing lustily twenty-nine times, mongrels in the morning, the canoodling of pigeons, the tide coming into the town of ghosts (population 2,000); 1601 was but yesterday, and spooks abound. Joy-bells ring for living and drowned (the Irish life underneath the waves); when the tide goes out and the wind drops there'll be a couple of jumps.

A bitch in heat is being chased through the flat of town by six mongrels anxious to cover her, despite newly enacted by-laws for the control of wandering pets; but ours was ever a country notoriously difficult to control. Windblown pines, surging ambient darkness.

From 'Sodden Fieltls', published in **Flotsam & Jetsam** *(Minerva, 1997; Dalkey Archive Press, 2002), a collection of shorter fiction by Aidan Higgins.*

The Old Fort, Kinsale

A Valentine card from the Adrian Healy collection showing the Old Fort in Kinsale. There are three former military forts in Kinsale, this, the ruins of the old medieval fort which was occupied by the Spanish in 1601 – supporting the Ulster earls in the Nine Years War (opposing Elizabethan inroads into Ireland) – James Fort which was built during the reign of James I, and, thirdly, Charles Fort, which was built in the 1670s and 1680s (and continued in service until the 1920s), named in honour of Charles II. This card was posted in Kinsale in October 1906, to Herbert Alcock Esq, Ingleside, Highams Park, Chingford, Essex, England, the card (which is very difficult to make out because it is written with some kind of thick marker) reads: "Glad to get a letter. You did not enclose the messial. Great check to <<*illegible*>> -ward. I think I would have returned it. We have not yet got our <<*cannot make out four words*>> here yesterday but had another enjoyment. Love to my niece, Moriarty."

Military Barracks, Kinsale

A postcard from the John James collection published by John O'Sullivan of Market Street, Kinsale – a tobacconist's – showing part of the British military barracks at Kinsale The card was never posted, nevertheless it is print-stamped '16 May 1920' (which is not, however, a post office stamp).

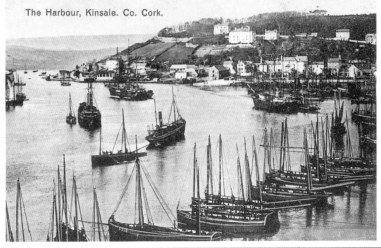

The Harbour, Kinsale. Co. Cork.

Two postcards from the John James collection showing the Kinsale quaysides: the black and white card (**above**) is a Lawrence card; the coloured card has no publisher statement. Neither card was posted.

THE QUAY, KINSALE

Street View, Kinsale

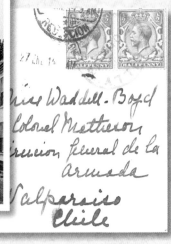

A Valentine card from the John James collection showing part of Fisher Street; the card was posted in London to a Miss Waddell-Boyd, c/o Colonel Matheson, Direccion General de la Armada, Valparaiso, Chile: "So glad to have a line from you & to hear you are better. I heard of your illness from the Dormans & was so sorry – Very best wishes for this New Year, with love from Mary E Nesbett."

KINSALE, Co. CORK.

From the John James collection, this view of Kinsale Harbour was published by E. T. W. Dennis & Sons, Ltd., of London and Scarborough. This card was never posted.

Also from the John James collection, this card shows part of Long Quay, which is the main street, or orientation point, in Kinsale. This postcard has no publisher statement and was never posted.

LONG QUAY, KINSALE

THE LONG QUAY, KINSALE

A Fergus O'Connor card from the Adrian Healy collection showing the reverse view of Long Quay. This postcard was never posted. On the B-side of this card someone has written "Murphy's Hotel facing camera."

THE OLD CHURCHYARD, INNISHANNON

From the John James collection, a postcard showing the ruins of St Mary's (old church) in Innishannon, posted in Kinsale in 1960 to a Madame Golduer (or possibly 'Goldeier') at 4 Square Claude Debussy, Paris. After dating the communication – 1 September 1960 – the communication reads: "Nous espêrons que vous avez eu des vacances et un repos aussi agreeable que nous dans ce joli coin d'Irelande – chere Madame – D'Armand et moi mos bonnes pensés, Madeleine Dubois" [We hope that you have had rest and holidays as agreeable as we have had in this beautiful part of Ireland – Dear Madame – from Armand and me, Best Wishes, Madeleine Dubois]. There is no publisher statement.

Downdaniel Castle, Bandon.   1368.

From the Adrian Healy collection, a card showing the ruins of Downdaniel Castle on the banks of the Bandon river, about halfway between Bandon and Innishannon. Downdaniel (also sometimes 'Dundaniel') dates from the 1460s and has been the possession of a succession power groups – the Barry Oges, the McCarthy Reaghs, Richard Boyle (the first earl of Cork) and sons, and even the East India Company – who were interested in the surrounding woodlands for ship-building and iron-ore-smelting. The postcard has no publisher statement and was never posted.

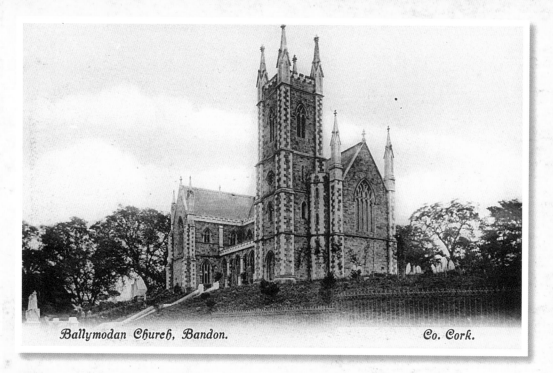

Ballymodan Church, Bandon.   *Co. Cork.*

Above: From the John James collection a Lawrence postcard showing St Peter's, Ballymodan, the Anglican church in Bandon, built in the 1840s (rebuilt on the site of an older Anglican church building). This card was never posted.

Below: From the Adrian Healy collection a Lawrence card showing Castle Bernard, home and fortress of the earls of Bandon, burned down during the War of Independence in 1921. This card was posted in Bandon on 23 December 1905 to Mrs Tighe, Woodstock, Inistioge, Co. Kilkenny: "With our greetings and best wishes for Xmas and New Year."

Castle Bernard, Bandon.   *Co. Cork.*

BANDON.

Ja-Ja
REG?
TRADE MARK.
HERALDIC SERIES.

From the John James collection, a Ja-Ja "Heraldic Series" postcard showing the coat of arms (or town crest) for Bandon – 'Bandon Bridge' as the town was known for many years. 'Ja-Ja' is a trademark registered in 1905 by Stoddart & Co., of Halifax in Yorkshire, England. This card was never posted.

No houses to let, but this chap will find you Lodgings.

At Bandon.

From the Adrian Healy collection, this "National Series" postcard was (apparently) sent to a Miss Rita Lawton of Bridge Street, Bandon; the message reads "Hope he will visit you soon" and is signed "A friend." The card is stamped with a tangerine coloured one penny George V stamp (*circa* 1912-24), however the stamp is uncancelled, therefore, if the card was delivered it was not by way of the postal service. "National Series" was a trademark of Millar & Lang Limited, printers and publishers with premises in London and Glasgow.

Facing page: From the Adrian Healy collection, a postcard showing Bandon Bridge spanning the Bandon River, published by S. O'Farrell of 87 South Main Street, Bandon. In the right side of the picture can be seen part of the Methodist church building in Bandon (dating from 1822). This postcard was never posted.

Above: From the John James collection, a Valentine card showing Coolfadda Mills on the riverbank of the Bandon river – from the 1800s to the 1960s this mill building was successively a woollen mill, a cotton mill, and a flour mill. This card was never posted.

Below: From the Adrian Healy collection, a Lawrence postcard showing Bandon's South Main Street, the town's main commercial thoroughfare. 'W. & G. Bright, Bandon' is also printed on the reverse of this card, which was never posted.

BANDON BRIDGE.

THE TRADE of the town itself had wonderfully increased. The wool of countless flocks of sheep passed through the hands of the wool-comber, the weaver, the dyer, the cloth-worker, and, finally, of the clothier – who shipped it to England or to foreign markets, and brought back money in its stead. Herds of well-bred cattle also contributed to the wealth of the country. There were butchers and victuallers to dispose of their meat, comb-makers and chandlers to manufacture combs and candles out of the bones and fat; and very numerous tanneries, where the tanner and the currier converted their hides into leather, most of which obtained a market elsewhere, and what was left the saddler and the cordwainer turned to profitable account.

Other trades were here also, whose very presence was indicative of the well-being of the inhabitants. There were goldsmiths, to provide gold rings and chains for our Bandon fair; glovers to supply them with gloves, perfumes, and the other requisites of the toilet; apothecaries and chirurgeons, to mix a posset and to bleed the sick; malsters, to supply materials for home-brewed ale; and millers to grind the corn into flour for bread-cakes. There were inn-holders, in whose hostelries the townsman could regale himself with prawns and broiled oysters, and wash them down with the pottle of sack. There were gardeners to supply his wife with a nosegay; and musicians, to the music of whose lute or spinet he could dance a saraband or a minuet, or accompany with some roundelay which he had learned in his infancy among the orchards of Somersetshire or Devon.

There were members of other trades, too, to supply the requirements of our thriving town. There were bakers, stainers, carpenters, glaziers, blacksmiths, mettlemen, coopers, masons, tailors, feltmakers, pewtermen, barbers, salters, parchment-makers, cutlers, &c., &c.

From George Bennett's **History of Bandon, and of the Principal Towns in the West Riding of County Cork** *(1869).*

From the Adrian Healy collection, a postcard published by E. Carroll Dawson of Bandon showing the British army garrison on parade. This card was never posted.

A Lawrence postcard from the John James collection, showing (left to right) Bandon Town Hall, the Courthouse, and the Masonic Hall (No. 84, or 'Antient Boyne'). This card was never posted.

From the Adrian Healy collection, a postcard showing Bridge Street, Bandon, published by S. O'Farrell of 87 South Main Street. This postcard was never posted

A David Cole postcard from the John James collection. This card was never posted. On the reverse is printed: 'Two contestants bowl an iron ball along the road. The winner is the one who completes a measured course with the least number of throws. Many bets are placed before the contest and great skill is needed by the bowlers. Played mainly in Cork and Armagh [in Northern Ireland]. The bowlers [pictured] are Denis Carroll (left) and Peter Farrell (right). A limited edition postcard, No. 6 in the Irish Series, photographed and published by David Cole.'

Enniskeane and Ballineen are twin villages 15 and 16 kilometres west of Bandon, Ballineen the further west of the two. This Ballineen postcard is from the John James collection. It does not have a publisher statement, and the card was never posted.

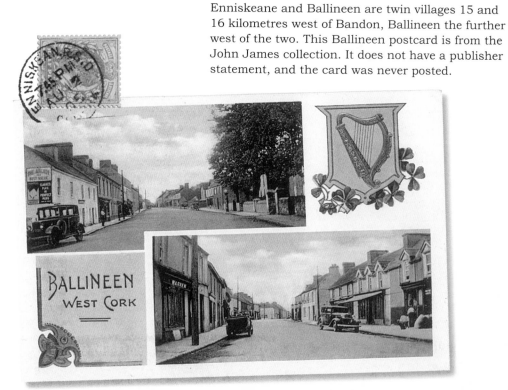

From the Adrian Healy collection, a John Hinde postcard showing a modern street-view of Bandon (Oliver Plunkett Street); photography by Dieter Boehm and Andrea Harmssen. This postcard was never posted.

© John Hinde Irreland Ltd.

CO. CORK

COURTMACSHERRY

From the Adrian Healy collection, an Insight Ireland postcard offering a composite of Courtmacsherry scenes (photography by Peter Zöller) – Courtmacsherry is a little seaside village on the south side of Courtmacsherry Bay, which is 10 kilometres south of Bandon. This postcard was never posted.

From the John James collection, a postcard of Kilbrittain Castle published by E. C. Dawson of Bandon. This postcard was never posted. Kilbrittain Castle, which is seven or eight kilometres south of Bandon, is said to be the oldest continuously inhabited castle in Ireland – originally dating from, it is believed, the 11th century.

Another E. C. Dawson card from the John James collection. Forming part of Courtmacsherry Bay, Harbour View is ten kilometres south of Bandon. Posted in Courtmacsherry in September [1906?] this postcard was sent to W. H. Lackland Esq., at "Sunnyside", Eccleston Park, Preston, Lancashire, England: "We are having very nice weather. Kilbrittain is very like St Bees. There is Golf, Fishing (Sea), Boating, nice walks and drives, and very quiet. Hoping you are well, TM."

WHEN THE ABBEY was in its glory, when those ivy-mantled ruins, now tenanted by the bat and the owl, were occupied by numerous Franciscan friars, it must have been delightful – at full tide, on a waning summer's evening – to listen to the vesper-hymn pouring from out the painted windows of the cloister, and rolling with melodious swell down through the echoing woods which at that time embosomed the estuary of the Arigadeen; and listen on, and hear the last lingering note grow soft and faint – and yet softer and fainter still – as it slowly crept along to the great ocean that lay asleep outside the dark cliffs of Lislee.

From George Bennett's **History of Bandon, and of the Principal Towns in the West Riding of County Cork** *(1869).*

Timoleague Castle.   Co. Cork.

Timoleague Abbey.

Above left: A postcard from the John James collection offering an artist's sketch of the ruins of the old Franciscan abbey at Timoleague. The abbey was established as a Franciscan foundation in the 1240s on the site of a monastic settlement founded by St Molaga in the 6th century. 'Timoleague' comes from the Gaelic for House of Molaga, Tigh Mologa. The artist has not been identified (the sketch is signed "B.D."); there is no publisher's statement on this postcard and it was never posted. **Above right:** A Lawrence postcard from the Adrian Healy collection showing the tower house that is Timoleague Castle. This card was never posted: "The town of Timoleague, and much of the adjacent country, anciently belonged to the Hodnetts – an English family who settled here from Shopshire [in Norman times]; and prior to their advent it belonged to the O'Cowigs," says George Bennett in his *History of Bandon* (pp. 355-7). The Barrymores then became its owners, and they and their descendants retained possession of it until some years since, when it was purchased by the late Colonel Travers. The same authority states that the castle is "said to be built by the Morils, in 1206" (*ibid*, p. 356 footnote). The tennis courts in the bottom right corner of the picture are the original courts of the Argideen Vale Lawn Tennis and Croquet Club whose first recorded club president was Robert Augustus Travers of Timoleague Castle.

From the John James collection, an R. A. Publishing Company postcard of Main Street, Clonakilty (Radermacher, Aldous, & Co., Ludgate Hill, London – the company supplied cards to small retailers and printed their customer's names as the publisher, in this case J. E. Spiller, Sovereign Street, Clonakilty). This postcard was never posted.

From the Adrian Healy collection, a contemporary Insight Ireland postcard showing the market town of Clonakilty nestled in its rich agricultural hinterland (photography by Peter Zöller). This card was never posted.

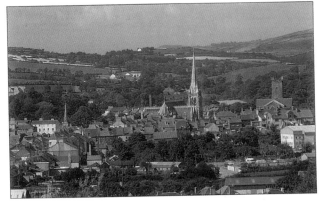

CLONAKILTY

Main Street, Clonakilty.

From the John James collection, Main Street, Clonakilty – again – almost the very same view as the card above, but on Fair Day – another J. E. Spiller postcard. This card was posted in August 1910, to Mrs A. Daniel, 28 Fourth Avenue, Queen's Park, London: "I expect to be home on the 30th. Shall hope to come and see you one day. Will any day do? How about tues? Yours T.T.M."

The Convent, Clonakilty, Co. Cork.

From the John James collection, a Lawrence postcard of the Convent of Mercy, Clonakilty, posted in June 1907 to a Miss MacDonnell at Lee Villa, Sunday's Well, Cork: "17 Sovereign Street, Clonakilty, June 3rd '07 | Get M.A.P. for 1st June and look at page 562 and you will be charmed. I hope you got home alright yesterday. With love, B. Patten."

From the Adrian Healy collection, a J. E. Spiller postcard of the Tadhg O'Donovan Asna monument in Clonakilty. Tadhg O'Donovan Asna led the only United Irishmen uprising in Munster (the United Irishmen of 1798 were inspired by the American and French Revolutions). The monument, which is at the corner of modern-day Ashe and Astna streets, was commissioned in 1898 to commemorate the United Irishmen and the centenary of 1798.

98 Monument, Clonakilty.

Clonakilty, County Cork, Ireland

A Mac Publications postcard from the Adrian Healy collection showing the houses on one side of Emmet Square in Clonakilty. The Emmet Square houses were built between 1785 and 1810; originally the square was Shannon Square, after the earls of Shannon (descendents of Richard Boyle, the first earl of Cork), but was renamed Emmet Square in the Nationalist Era in honour of Robert Emmet, a United Irishman executed by the British authorities in 1803. This postcard was never posted.

A J. E. Spiller card from the Adrian Healy collection showing a market-day scene on George Street, Clonakilty (George Street is now Connolly Street). This postcard was never posted.

INCHYDONEY HOTEL, CLONAKILTY, CO. CORK.

From the John James collection, a Real Photo by Mason, Dublin, showing the old Inchydoney Hotel on Inchydoney Island in Clonakilty Bay (the Inchydoney Hotel has since been completely rebuilt and is now the Inchydoney Lodge and Spa). The card was posted to the 'Misses Doyle' at 11 Duke Street, Dublin: "Having a lovely time. See you when I return next week, Love Vera." This communication is not dated and the stamp and cancellation postmark on the card have been damaged so that it is not possible to say when (precisely) the card was posted.

IT IS A MOST exciting summer's day: live wind, the sea all agog. But for the moon's leash it would leap ashore and carry us all away.

Jack and Nanny and Baby and Amy, the nursery maid, and myself are having tea on the strand, with scalding hot tea in an iron kettle wrapped in many newspapers.

"Here's a lady's seat", Jacky says, indicating a rock. "Sit down, my dear creature, and enjoy yourself."

Baby takes off his floppy hat and sits with bare head, bald and seal-like, scrabbling his toes in the dry sand. The donkey, tied to the gate, is asleep, swaying gently in the shafts.

Battery people on their way back from a funeral at Ross pass by in their carts. The men have drink taken. They snatch off their hats with a flourish and pass on.

Jacky and I see how unusual the sea is, how alive and splendid it is in its green and silver brightness.

"Was it on a day like this, do you know, that the Spanish Armada ship went down on the Dulig?" Jacky points to the black rock where the waves are tossing spray.

"No one knows. It might have been in a bright blue and white gale, or in an angry black and purple storm, or in an inky mist at night. Anyhow, the ship hurled herself on the sword of Dulig and perished."

"What a waste!" Jacky said. "Poor drowned men! How nothing they are!"

Mary Carbery's **West Cork Journal, 1898-1901,** *edited by Jeremy Sandford (Lilliput Press, 1998).*

Castle Freke, Clonakilty

From the John James collection, a J. E. Spiller card of Castlefreke, home and estate of the Barons Carbery up until the 1919 when, following a fire, it was sold by the 10th Lord Carbery, John Evans-Freke (1892-1970). This postcard was posted in Hinckley in Leicestershire in May 1913 to a Miss A. Harrington, at 42 Duncan Terrace, Islington, London: "Arrived here this morning and had a very nice journey over. Am getting the fine weather now that my holidays are coming to an end. Will get back to London some time on Monday and shall probably see you if I am not too tired. Best love, Willie."

Owenahincha Strand, Rosscarbery, Co. Cork, Ireland.   Photo: D. Noble, John Hinde Studios.

A John Hinde card from the Adrian Healy collection (photography by D. Noble). The card was never posted. On the reverse the John Hinde company have the following note about the Castlefreke-Owenahincha-Rosscarbery stretch of coastline (which is 10 kilometres west of Clonakilty): "Situated on Rosscarbery Bay, Owenahincha is a charming, secluded seaside resort with an abundance of uncrowded and unspoilt beach. Nearby is Castlefreke ancestral home of Lord Carbery, who renounced the peerage in 1926. The small town of Rosscarbery occupies an elevated position and is an ideal spot for a quiet holiday. Records tell that in the sixth century St Fachnan founded in Rosscarbery a monastery, which became famous for its school."

From the John James collection a postcard showing the village of Rosscarbery published by J. H. Audley of Passage West. This card was posted to a Mrs A. Turner, Jalna, 8 Dundela Avenue, Sandycove, Dublin: "This is a delightful little place – so far we've had wonderful weather. Michael has caught quite a few trout, & young Mick caught a bass! With love & best wishes to you both, Michael, Margaret, & family."

A Lawrence card from the Adrian Healy collection showing Derry House, west of Rosscarbery, which was owned by Charlotte [*née* Townshend] wife of the playwright George Bernard Shaw. This card was posted in Rosscarbery in January 1920 to a Miss Julia <<*most of the address is whited out*>> Bandon, County Cork: "Dear Julia," the writer begins "your letter to hand: glad to hear you are coming. Hoping the day will be fine. Why not P. come? You did not say how you would come. I'm longing to see you. Good bye for the present, love from Bridie." The communication is dated "3/1/'20."

From the John James collection a postcard of Mount St Michael Convent School, Rosscarbery. There is no publisher statement on this card. It was posted in Rosscarbery in May 1910 to a Mrs Scanlon, Main Street, Dungarvan, Co. Waterford: "Dear Mrs Scanlon, kindly pray and get all the prayers you can for our beloved M. de Salis, who is in a very critical state. The Drs have very little hope of her. Yours affectionately, Str M. Gonzaga."

From the Adrian Healy collection an Insight Ireland postcard of the Bronze Age Drombeg Stone Circle, near Glandore. This card has not been posted.

© John Hinde Irreland Ltd.

Village of Glandore, West Cork

Also from the Adrian Healy collection, a John Hinde postcard view of the pier area in the village of Glandore (photography by D. Noble). This postcard was never posted.

Rineen Mill, Co. Cork.

And again from the Adrian Healy collection, a Lawrence card of the grain mill at Rineen, which is at the north-western corner of Castletownshend Harbour. This postcard was posted in Glandore in August 1906, sent to a Miss Phillips at Orchard House, Dartford, Kent, in England: "Am down here for a few days rest", the sender, Mr Dennis J. O'Neill, begins, "It is just lovely, so quiet. Regards, Dennis J. O'Neill, Bantry."

From the John James collection, a Lawrence postcard showing the old driveway into Myross Wood, which at the time was a Townshend property – cousins of the Townshends that owned Derry House, Rosscarbery (see p. 78) – today Myross Wood is a Missionaries of the Sacred Heart retreat centre. On the card it states that this is a Lawrence picture and the postcard was published by Wolfe Brothers, Skibbereen, however, in reality Wolfe is only retailing what is wholly a Lawrence production. This postcard was posted in May 1907 to a Miss P. Dailey, Ferney, Stillorgan, Dublin: "This view is the avenue of the place we stayed on Monday night", the sender writes. "An arm of the sea is within a stone's throw of the left side. Much love, Yours, J."

From the John James collection, a postcard of the village of Leap, near Skibbereen, published by Wolfe Bros., Main Street, Skibbereen. On the reverse is written: "Passed through this little town by bus, it was lovely", however the postcard is not post office stamped in any way so the card may have been an enclosure in another communication.

From the Adrian Healy collection, an Avon Sales card showing the Ilen River valley (with the town of Skibbereen nestled in the distance – centre of the picture). Posted in Longford in August 1984, to a Mrs Mackay at Cairearn, Drunanadrochit, near Inverness, in Scotland: "Having a lovely time" the sender writes, "and weather very good. All quite expert at the boat handling now. Managed to see quite a lot of places. Love Ina & Gordon."

From the Adrian Healy collection, a postcard showing Raheen Castle, Myross, which is on the eastern shoreline of Castlehaven (or Castletownshend) Harbour. This card has not been posted and there is no publisher statement. There is, however, a 'K Ltd' logo in the stamp box area (with the 'K' overlaid on the 'Ltd'), but, apparently, this is not a postcard publisher's trademark, it has to do with the photographic paper used in making the postcard. '1938' is written on the reverse of the card (top left) in black ink, and beneath it, in another hand, 'Co. Cork', in pencil. The car is a 1936 Ford 10. Raheen (or Rahine) Castle is a tower house built by Donell O'Donovan of Castledonovan in the 1580s.

CASTLETOWNSHEND

West Cork

Never posted, an Insight Ireland postcard of Castletownshend from the Adrian Healy collection (photography by Peter Zöller). Castletownshend is 10 kilometres south-east of Skibbereen.

Glen Barrahane, Castletownshend.

From the John James collection, a postcard of Glen Barrahane, Castletownshend, published by Wolfe Bros., Main Street, Skibbereen. Glen Barrahane was where Admiral Somerville was murdered by a renegade IRA unit in 1936 (Henry Boyle Townshend Somerville, 1863-1936, brother of the writer Edith Somerville, 1858-1949).

Two cards from the Adrian Healy collection, (**above**) a postcard showing the Ilen River and the town of Skibbereen, published in the C. H. Webb Series, and (**below**) a view of Bridge Street, Skibbereen, looking west (the structure on the left with the arch is the old entrance to the Fairfield; a little further on is the entrance to the Abbeystrewry Church of Ireland). The Bridge Street postcard was published by D. O'Connell of Skibbereen. Neither of these postcards was posted.

Facing page: From the John James collection, a Hartmann postcard showing the Town Hall in Skibbereen; 'Guy & Co., Ltd' is also printed on the reverse, so presumably the postcard was locally published by the Francis Guy company, stationers and publishers of St Patrick Street, Cork. This postcard was never posted.

Market Square, Skibbereen.

Main Street, Skibbereen, Co. Cork.

Above: From the Adrian Healy collection, a postcard of the view down Main Street, Skibbereen – looking west – with, in the foreground, the Maid of Erin monument commemorating the several militarized nationalist campaigns in Ireland, published by Wolfe Bros., Skibbereen (a Lawrence photo). This card was never posted. **Below:** From the John James collection, a C. H. Webb postcard of the Provincial Bank on North Street, Skibbereen. This card was never posted.

Provincial Bank Skibbereen.

C.H.Webb's Series

A GREY FIGURE still marks the heart of Skibbereen, a statue of the Maid of Erin. It's in the way, but has been decreed by referendum to remain. Around it the shops are modest for the most part, the banks big, the bars frequent: a good business town, my father used to say. Memory focusses here, the dredged-up images are clearer. Horses and carts in the narrow streets, with milk churns for the creamery. On fair-days farmers with sticks standing by their animals, their shirts clean for the occasion, without collar or tie. A smell of whiskey, and sawdust and stout and dung. Pots of geraniums among the chops and ribs in the small windows of the butchers' shops. A sun-burnt poster, advertising the arrival of Duffy's Circus a year ago.

It was a mile and a half, the journey to school through the town, past Driscoll's sweetshop and Murphy's Medical Hall, and Power's drapery, where you could buy oilcloth as well as dresses. You made the journey home again at three. By three on fair-days the buying and selling was over, the publicans' takings safely banked, the dung sliding towards the gutters. If you had money you spent it on liquorice pipes or stuff for making lemonade, which was delicious if you ate it just as it was. The daughters of Power's drapery sometimes had money. But they were always well ahead, on bicycles because they were well-to-do. On fair-days their mother drove them in her Hillman because of the dung.

In the grocers' shops the big-jawed West Cork women buy flour and sausages and tins of plums, and trade their baskets of turkey eggs. E. O'Donovan, undertaker, still sells ice-cream and chocolate. The brass plate of Redmond O'Regan, solicitor, once awkwardly high, is now below eye-level, and Shannon's bakery has a café, where commercial travellers hurry through their cups of tea or coffee. Mr Dwyer, who bred smooth-haired fox-terriers, used to serve in Shannon's, expertly tying up pounds of sugar and tea in grey paper-bags. We bought a dog from him once, an animal called Dano who became infatuated with our cat.

The door beside the Methodist church, once green, is purple. The church, small and red-brick, stands behind high iron railings and gates, with gravel in front of it. Beyond the door that used to be green is the dank passage that leads to Miss Willoughby's schoolroom, where first I learnt that the world is not an easy-going place. Miss Willoughby was stern and young, in love with the cashier from the Provincial Bank. Like the church beside her schoolroom, she was Methodist and there burnt in her breast an evangelical spirit which stated that we, her pupils, except for her chosen few, must somehow be made less wicked than we were. Her chosen few were angels of a kind, their handwriting blessed, their compositions a gift from God. I was not among them.

On the gravel in front of the red-brick church I vividly recall Miss Willoughby. Terribly, she appears. Severe and beautiful, she pedals against the wind on her huge black bicycle. "Someone laughed during prayers", her stern voice accuses, and you feel at once that it was you, although you know it wasn't. 'V. poor' she writes in your headline book when you've done your best to reproduce, four times, perfectly, 'Pride goeth before destruction.'

As I stand on the gravel, her evangelical eyes seem again to dart over me without pleasure. Once I took the valves out of the tyres of her bicycle. Once I looked in her answer book. "Typical", her spectre says. "Typical, to come prying." I am late, I am stupid. I cannot write twenty sentences on 'A Day in the Life of an Old Shoe', I cannot do simple arithmetic or geography, I am always fighting with Jasper Swanton. I move swiftly on the gravel, out on to the street and into the bar of the Eldon Hotel: in spectral form or otherwise, Miss Willoughby will not be there.

From William Trevor's **Excursions in the Real World** *(Hutchinson, 1993).*

NORTH STREET, SKIBBEREEN, CO. CORK

Above: From the Adrian Healy collection, a Cardall postcard of North Street, Skibbereen, which is from the late 1950s or early 1960s. The card was posted in Skibbereen on 19 August 1961, to J. Ruane at 1 Edward Street, Brighouse, Yorkshire, in England: "Only done 43 miles today," the writer, Billy, says, "the wind is fairly strong. Anyway, I stopped at the first hotel I came across, the Eldon, the second good place so far. The evening is coming in cold and I hope it does not rain. I am waiting for grilled trout. Love, Billy."

Below: Also from the Adrian Healy collection, a Lawrence postcard of the Convent of Mercy in Skibbereen. This postcard was never posted, however, on the reverse the card is date-stamped '1 Jun 1963' (not a post office stamp).

Convent of Mercy, Skibbereen, Co. Cork.

Facing page: From the John James collection, an E. Mack card posted in 1915, to a Miss Betty Adams, The Nest, Avendale Road, Littleham, Nr Exmouth, in Devon in England: "To wish you a Happy Easter. From Harry."

Grub's Going Up !
at SKIBBEREEN.

Creagh Church.   *Skibbereen, Co. Cork.*

From the Adrian Healy collection, a postcard of Creagh Church on the southern bank of the Ilen River, between Skibbereen and Baltimore. This card was posted in Skibbereen in July 1903 (or possibly 1905), to a Mrs J. W. Bennett at Millville in Clonakilty: "Did you read Willie's letter, it was asking for more strawberries as Mrs E. is fond of them. Did Dr Jack see Tom. How are you all getting on, I suppose Emily did not turn up yet. Aunt Eva is still away Ellie & Mrs Ware coming to-night. Yours lovingly, Saidie."

© John Hinde Ireland Ltd.

Lough Ine near Skibbereen, Co. Cork, Ireland.   Photo: D. Noble, John Hinde Studios.

From the Adrian Healy collection, a John Hinde postcard of Lough Ine (Lough Hyne), near Skibbereen, which is a salt-water lake (photography by D. Noble). This card was never posted. On the reverse the John Hinde company has the following note: "Lough Ine, near Skibbereen, Co. Cork. Skibbereen is one of the principal towns of Co. Cork and is built on the River Ilen, where it widens out to form a creek and unites its waters with an inlet of Baltimore Bay. Lough Ine, a beautiful land-locked inlet surrounded by hills, is situated 4½ miles south of Skibbereen. On an islet in the centre of the lough stand the fragmentary remains of Lough Ine Castle, an old fortress of the O'Driscolls."

From the Adrian Healy collection, a Lawrence postcard of Baltimore, southwest of Skibbereen. This card was posted in Baltimore in September 1908, to Mrs A. Harris at 12 Windsor Terrace, Jenkins Street, Small Heath, Birmingham, England: "Dear Art, We return back on Friday so I will come & see you Sunday week. Love to all, in haste, Floss xxxxxx."

From the Adrian Healy collection, a Lawrence postcard showing the ruins of the Franciscan abbey on Sherkin Island in Baltimore Harbour. The card was posted to a Miss M. K. Symes, at the Bank of Ireland in Skibbereen in October 1903: after dating the card "31.10.1903", the sender, Ina A. Symes, continues: "I hope you will not mind, but I am sending B. Castle to Sisse here as you said you did not want it sent to you. You see it would be a pity to waste such a pretty one. Thank you." And, written on the picture side, "I wonder how many of the wishes wished here come true. Love from Ina A. Symes." Sherkin Abbey was a Franciscan foundation built in the 1480s with the patronage of the O'Driscolls of Baltimore, the local clan-based power group.

Fish Market. Baltimore.

From the Adrian Healy collection, a postcard showing a fish market scene on the pier at Baltimore, published by Hely's Limited, Dublin. This postcard was never posted. The children in this picture are, apparently, inmates of the Baltimore Industrial School, notorious for its harshness towards and neglect of the innocents in its care – for an account of which, see Alfred O'Mahony's *The Way We Were* (Inspire Books, 2011).

NORTH PIER, CAPE CLEAR. CO. CORK.

From the John James collection, a postcard of the North Pier, Cape Clear Island, published in C. H. Webb's Series, Ballydehob. The card was posted in 1905 to Miss M. K. Symes, at the Bank of Ireland in Skibbereen: "Just outside Ballybrophy where we had to change with <<*words illegible*>> to Wall.carriage, <<*word illegible*>> a very good <<*illegible*>>. Got <<*illegible*>> saw Jo. All well. Love to each, M."

From the Adrian Healy collection, a card showing women working at fish curing on the pier at Cape Clear Island, a postcard from Hely's Limited, Dublin. This postcard was posted in Enniskeane in August 1905 to a Miss Kathleen Gilpin, C/o Mrs Dole in Dunmanway: "Could you or any of the others ride tomorrow, Tuesday."

Fish Curing — Cape Clear.

DURNING THE SUMMER months the native fishermen man their hookers and boats, and nearly all the adult population weigh anchor every Monday or Tuesday morning, and proceed far out to sea – the hookers steering for the Durseys, and the open boats for the neighbourhood of the Fastnett. Sometimes, in pursuit of their calling, they go thirty leagues off the land; they remain out during the week, and return on Friday or Saturday with their cargoes of hake, ling, codfish, congers, and other deep sea fish on board, then they anchor near St Kieran's strand, and soon the beach is covered with the captured spoil of the finny tribe.

The scene which ensues is most interesting and exciting; all the female population rush to the beach, attended by the "gorsoons," and soon the fish are packed in baskets, which they swing upon their shoulders with the greatest ease, and carry away up the steep and slippery pathways of the island. The women are engaged then in curing the fish, a process which is accomplished with great skill; and the men rest for a couple of days to recruit themselves for further expeditions out to sea. As the agricultural produce of the island is comparatively small, chiefly oats and potatoes, and as all fuel must be brought from the mainland, there being no trees or turf on the soil, it is evident that not alone their welfare but also their principal means of procuring a livelihood depend on the success of the fisheries. The chief time of the year for disposing of the cured fish is at Christmas, when very large quantities are sold, especially in the town of Skibbereen.

From Daniel Donovan's **Sketches in Carbery** *(1876).*

MAIN STREET, BALLYDEHOB.

C. H. Webb's

Two Ballydehob postcards from the Adrian Healy collection. **Above:** A street scene on Main Street, Ballydehob, a card published by C.H. Webb. This postcard (which is physically damaged) was posted in Ballydehob in September 1905, to a Miss Aileen Attridge at Coolagh, Ballydehob: "Dearest Aileen," the writer – Julie – begins, "Thanks for yours. I am very sorry as [I can't] go to you [because] Mrs FitzGerald will be in Schull the whole day tomorrow and I must stay to mind baby. But perhaps we will have some other day together soon. Give my love to all. I am, dearest, yours as ever, Julie." **Below:** A John Hinde postcard of Ballydehob in the 1970s (photography by D. Noble). This card was never posted.

Ballydehob Village, West Cork, Ireland.

Photo: D. Noble, John Hinde Studios.

Two postcards of Schull from the Adrian Healy collection. **Above:** A Regatta Day postcard published by D. Newman. This card was posted in July 1958 to a Miss M. McCormack at Carrowmore, Ballina, Co Mayo: "12/7/58 | Inglenook | Schull | Co Cork | Hope you are all in excellent form. I am enjoying this place very much & we even have a lovely little church. Much love to all, Alice C."

Below: A street scene on Main Street, Schull. A KenCard Series card, produced by Kennelly Photoworks, Ashe Street, Tralee (photography by Padraig Kennelly). This card was posted in Skibbereen on 19 August 1961, to J. Ruane at 1, Edward Street, Brighouse, Yorkshire in England: "Sat in sun on past this place. It is a wild place but there seems to be plenty of people about. Love, Billy."

MAIN STREET, SCHULL, CO. CORK.

Two cards from the Adrian Healy collection. **Above:** A John Eagle postcard of Mizen Head Signal Station, Crookhaven. **Below:** A postcard of Heron's Cove, Goleen, published by Sue Hill's Heron's Cove B & B and Restaurant (photography by John Eagle). Neither of these postcards has been posted.

The Heron's Cove

Barleycove, Co.Cork

Two cards from the Adrian Healy collection. **Above:** An Insight Ireland postcard of Barleycove near Crookhaven (photography by Peter Zöller). This card has not been posted. **Below:** A Lawrence postcard of Fastnet Lighthouse, which is 13 kms southwest of Ireland's mainland. One hundred and forty six feet high (44.5 m), with the focal point of the light 159 feet (48.5 m) above the high water mark. Fastnet Lighthouse was constructed in the 1890s and first lit in 1904. This postcard was posted in Queenstown [Cobh] in 1907, to a Mr M. White at Skirteen, Monasterevan, County Kildare: "Dear Brother, just a line to say that I got back allright, am writing from your B. JW."

Fastnet Lighthouse.   Co. Cork.

From the Adrian Healy collection, a John Hinde postcard of Allihies, which is at the western end of the Beara peninsula – about as far west as one can go in Ireland. On the reverse is the following note about Allihies and the surrounding district: 'Allihies, once the centre of a copper-rich district, is situated between Bantry Bay and the Kenmare River estuary on the Beara Peninsula – the most westerly of the long peninsulas of Cork. This region is almost entirely mountainous. The Caha and Slieve Miskish ranges form the mountain massif, and along the former range of mountains runs the border between Cork and Kerry.' The second card above is an Allihies postcard from the John James collection showing the villagers emerging from a church service. This card has no publisher statement and it was never posted.

ALLIHIES, WEST CORK

© John Hinde Ireland Ltd.

Facing page: From the Adrian Healy collection, a Lawrence card of Castletownbere and part of harbour area of Berehaven with Miskish Mountain in the background. This postcard was never posted. Castletownbere is also known as 'Castletown Berehaven', especially a century or so ago; however in modern usage the town is almost always Castletownbere, while 'Berehaven' usually refers to the waters of the harbour area.

Castletown Berehaven Co. Cork.

THIS IS THE road to Seal Harbour. That is the road to Zetland pier. Both names – not lying too easily with the older Gaelic names – are pretty obvious reminders that the British navy and its dependents spent a fair amount of time in the land of Beara who may have been a legendary princess from Spain who married into the people of this place long long before the Normans pushed the Sullivans south-west out of Tipperary. She may also never have existed, or simply have been the king of Spain's daughter who sat in the glow of a thousand hearths, moved through a thousand folk tales from the earliest times down to my late lamented friend, Mící Pháidi, in Rann na Feirsde in the Rosses of Donegal. Gap-toothed Mící could explain in detail how the king of Spain's daughter married a boyo who set out on his travels from Burtonport to the Indiacha Thoir, or East Indies, but who, regardless, ended up in Spain where he did well for himself and where he is to this day. At least he was there in the 1940s when Mící was alive:

Then the wet winding roads,
Brown bogs with black water,
And my thoughts on white ships
And the King of Spain's daughter.

… Nearly 35 years ago, and in the middle of a tempest, I came [to Castletownbere] for the first time and a young woman who had been talking to one of the Puxleys told me, among other things, the story of the four wild brothers from Adrigole.

What I remember most about that visit is (i) that it rained for three days and three nights (ii) that I was reading Maxim Gorki and (iii) that one of the two girls in the post-office had worn her way with her toenail through the toe of her right shoe. It was that girl or, perhaps, the other one who told me about the four wild brothers from Adrigole…

It rained, as I've said, for three days and three nights and the dark sky, driven like mad by a gale that came up and down the mountains from Kerry and Kenmare Bay, was so low you could have touched it if you cared to take the risk of bringing down worse on your head…

Thirteen trawlers from Bilbao were blown in out of the storm. The streets were crowed with little brown men, holy medals around their necks, deeply religious oaths on their lips, merriment and good nature in their eyes, bundles of silk stockings and bottles of quite lethal Iberian brandy under their oxters.

The stockings and the brandy they would barter for anything available. The dances in the hall beside the hotel were a sight to see. You wouldn't know under God what country you were in. And the rain rained and the wind blew and the sky licked the roofs of the houses: and I was reading Maxim Gorky. It's quite simple how I remember I was reading Gorky. It was that bit in his memoirs where he describes how the wooden houses went on fire in Osharsk Square in Nijhni Novgorod [afterwards Gorkigrad]. The fire crackled like an animal chewing bones. It made real comic reading when there you were and the heavens urinating on you at the far end of west Cork…

One evening when the rain was drawing its breath a bit I walked up and up the slope behind the church, up and up until I was out there on my own and the town well below me. The clouds came at me like buffaloes. To my right hand what would normally have been a simple mountain stream went down like Niagara towards the bay. It was a wonder all out that it didn't take the town with it. Oh far away was that animal of a fire in Osharsk Square, and I thought of Standish O'Grady and a little poem he had written about a mountain stream. After all, this was O'Grady's town, so I quoted him out loud to the torrent to remind it and the weather how they should behave themselves:

> *Cloud-begot, mountain-bred,*
> *Heather-nursed child,*
> *Innocent, beautiful,*
> *Winsome and wild.*

> *Here she comes dancing*
> *O'er boulder and rock,*
> *And in many a waterfall*
> *Shakes her white frock.*

A day and a half later the rain eased off: poetry is a slow-working charm. And one of the two girls who worked in the post office had worn her way with her toenail through the toe of her right shoe. She told me about this when she told me how she had been honoured to talk to one of the Puxleys of Dunboy when Brian Desmond Hurst and the actors and the cameraman were there, briefly, before working on the movie based on the DuMaurier novel [*Hungry Hill* (1943)]. There she was, she said, ashamed of her life, talking to Miss Puxley and her toe peeping out like a rabbit. So she put her left foot over the toes of her right foot and stood like that, balancing as well as she could until she noticed that the lady was balancing in the same way, except that her right foot was hiding the toes of her left foot: and the girl didn't know and never would whether there was or was not a hole also in the lady's shoe, or whether that was just the way the gentry stood, like herons, you know, or storks or flamingoes. She was a lively west Cork brunette and I'll never know whether or not she was making it all up. The other girl was blonde. It was a long time ago and, as I've said, you wouldn't have known, what with the rain and the men from Bilbao, what country you were in. Nor can I recall for certain which of the girls told me about the four wild brothers who lived according to instinct in the rocky wilderness of Adrigole.

*From Benedict Kiely's **All the way to Bantry Bay** (Victor Gollancz, 1978).*

Hotel and Main Street Castletown Berehaven, Co. Cork.

Above: From the Adrian Healy collection, a Lawrence card showing Main Street, Castletownbere, *circa* 1900, the Berehaven Hotel is on the right of the picture. This card was posted in Bantry in March 1905 to a Miss E. Prior at 12 Kensington Gardens, London. There was no written communication on the card sent to Miss Prior – the address is written in ink and in fine handwriting – however, apparently, the card was subsequently reused in another communication because in the space for the card's message (in pencil and in another hand – a poor hand) is written: "I am going to the pictures this evening with my girl." And, in yet another hand, also in pencil, someone added "So am I." **Below:** Another Lawrence postcard of a street scene in Castletownbere from the Adrian Healy collection. This card was never posted.

Middle Street Castletown Berehaven Co. Cork.

PULLEEN HARBOUR, BEREHAVEN, BANTRY BAY.

From the John James collection, a Fergus O'Connor card of Pulleen Harbour, which is five or six kilometres west of Castletownbere. This postcard was never posted.

The Church and Convent, Berehaven, Co. Cork.

From the Adrian Healy collection, a postcard of the Roman Catholic Sacred Heart church and convent in Castletownbere, published by D. D. Harrington, The Square, Castletownbere. This card was posted in Castletownbere in June 1931 to a Miss Girlie Kenny, at 28 Orwell Park, Rathgar, Dublin: "My dear Girlie", the writer begins "I was very glad to get your card and to see you are very well. Your writing is very good but write me a long letter next time. I hope you do not forget "Jinks." Marie was delighted with your badge, when she is big she will write to you. Shelia will show you Aunt Benignus's convent. I told her you are a very big girl now and very good at school. Best love from Margaret."

Druid Circle, Castletown, Berehaven

From the Adrian Healy collection, this postcard of the Druid Stone Circle ('Derrintaggert' or 'Derreenataggart' being the non-anglicized name for this Bronze Age feature) does not have a publisher statement. The card was posted in Castletownbere in July 1905, to a Mrs O'Dea at 12 Larne Terrace, North Circular Road, Dublin: "Dear Maggie", the sender begins underneath a "Castletownbere" place-statement, "I am here since Saturday & am going home on Tuesday. Love to all, Lucie." (Castletownbere is also known as 'Castletown Berehaven', especially a century or so ago; however in nowaday usage the town is almost always Castletownbere and Berehaven usually refers to the waters of the harbour area).

In Bantry Bay, Dunboy Castle, Berehaven.

From the Adrian Healy collection, a Fergus O'Connor postcard of Dunboy Castle (the Puxley place), Dunboy, Castletownbere. The Puxleys were landlords and mining magnates in the copper-rich Beara peninsula. The place was burned down in 1921 during the War of Independence. This postcard was posted in Portland Harbour in Dorset, England, in May 1911 to a Mr and Mrs Stripe at 28 Cambridge Street, Somers Road, Southsea, Hampshire: "Arrived at Portland at 10 o/c", the sender writes, "Will be leaving at 5.30 tomorrow & come in same day. Will write and catch first post in morning. With love & Best Wishes, GG Elson."

The Fleet at Castletown Berehaven, Co.Cork.

Postcards from the Adrian Healy collection showing British Royal Navy ships in Bantry Bay and Berehaven waters. 'Castletown Berehaven' – as it used to be called – was host to a Royal Navy squadron protecting the sea-routes to North America – a naval base of particular strategic significance during the First World War (1914-18). (It was in Berehaven waters that the fleet gathered before the Battle Jutland in 1916, the most significant navel engagment in the war.) Even after the War of Independence and the Anglo-Irish (peace) Treaty of 1921 Britain retained 'Castletown Berehaven' as one of the so-called 'Treaty Ports' (Haulbowline in Cork Harbour being another). Treaty Ports were finally handed over to the Irish state in 1938. This postcard (above) – a Lawrence card – was never posted.

Admirality Recreation Grounds Castletown Berehaven Co.Cork.

Also a Lawrence card from the Adrian Healy collection, a postcard showing the Admirality Recreation Grounds at the British Naval Base in Castletown Berehaven. On the reverse is written "With Love | From Vic" in ink. The card may have been an enclosure with a delivery – for example, it may have been used as a gift card.

From the Adrian Healy collection, this postcard was published by J. Flanagan of Castletownbere. It was posted to a Mrs Lee at Barna, Duxmere, Ross-on-Wye, Herefordshire, England: "I shall be returning on Sat 1st Sept", the writer – Michael – begins, "and would be very grateful if you could give me lunch that day. I hope to go on to Shropshire and spend the night with a friend but if that falls through I would very much like to spend the night with you. With love, Michael." Then a second person – Barbara – writes as follows at the very end of the message area of the card: "We hope to leave here on Sept 5th so would be with you on the 6th. We have had a bit of rain but it is fine today. Much love, Barbara."

A Fergus O'Connor card from the Adrian Healy collection: this card was posted at Waterfall, near Bantry, in April [1914?] to a Miss E. Bradford at 40 Waverly Road, Small Heath, Birmingham in England: "My Dear Sister", the writer begins below ranks of x's [representing kisses, 24 of them] "one or two for all", "I write these few lines to you hoping you are in the best of health as it leaves me at present. This is a postcard of the place where we are doing our ten weeks cruising and mine laying", and, following another line of x's, it is signed "Ted." Also written on a corner of the card is (presumably) Ted's address in Ireland: "15 Mess | H.M.S. Maid | Waterfall | Bantry | Ireland."

In Bantry Bay. Bere Island Ferry - Castletown - Berehaven.

From the Adrian Healy collection, a Fergus O'Connor postcard of the Bere Island Ferry. Bere Island is a large island (11 x 5 kilometres) located protectively in front of Castletownbere in Berehaven's waters (Bere Island is 1.5 kms from Castletownbere). The postcard has never been posted.

The Quay Bere Island Co. Cork.

From the Adrian Healy collection, a Lawrence postcard showing the Bere Island quayside. This card was posted in Bantry in December 1916 to a Mrs Carter at 18 Marlborough Road, Falmouth, Cornwall: "With best wishes to you all for Xmas & New Year", the writer – R. J. Forsdick – begins. "Hoping Major Carter is keeping well & that he will be home for Xmas. We are still here on this island which is very dull at present & fearfully bleak & cold. Hoping to hear from you soon. With love, R. J. Forsdick."

THE VILLAGE, BERE ISLAND, C? CORK

From the Adrian Healy collection, a Lawrence Photo postcard, published by D.D. Harrington of Castletownbere, of Rerrin (or Raerainn), the village on Bere Island. This postcard was never posted.

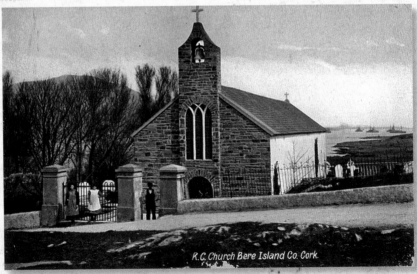

R.C. Church Bere Island Co. Cork.

The little Catholic church on Bere Island, St Michael's, which is at Ballinakilla. This is a Lawrence postcard from the Adrian Healy collection; the card was never posted.

Hungary Hill, Adrigole, Castletown, Berehaven.　　　Co. Cork.

From the John James collection, a Lawrence postcard of Hungry Hill, which has been described as 'an angry crouching animal of a mountain even in the morning sunlight' – Benedict Kiely in *All the Way to Bantry Bay* (1978). On the reverse of this postcard in green ink is written "In the southernmost county of Ireland." This card was never posted – at least, it is not addressed and it has never been stamped (it may have been an enclosure in another correspondence).

© John Hinde Ireland Ltd.

THE HEALY PASS, WEST CORK

From the Adrian Healy collection, a John Hinde postcard of the Healy Pass which traverses the Beara Peninsula (running north-south between Lauragh and Adrigole). The Healy Pass is named in honour of the journalist, barrister, and politician Timothy Michael Healy (1855-1931), a member of the House of Commons before independence (part of the so-called 'Bantry Gang') and first Governor-General of the Irish Free State. This postcard has never been posted.

Lord Bantry's Cottage
Glengarriff Co.Cork.

Above: From the John James collection, a Lawrence postcard of the hunting lodge of the earls of Bantry, which is three or four kilometres northwest of the village of Glengarriff (Glengarriff is about 15 kms from the town of Bantry – Bantry is on the south side of Bantry Bay, opposite Glengarriff on the north). This postcard was never posted. **Below:** Also from the John James collection, another Lawrence postcard: this tunnel goes through the Cork and Kerry mountains, constituting the border between the two counties. Unstamped, undated, and unsigned, this postcard was written for a Mr & Mrs Carvell at 344 Windmill Road, Ealing W.5, London: "This is where we went last Thursday", the writer writes, "it is a tunnel through the rocks which we had to go through. The treats are great that they are giving us & no expense to us & the chauffeur is very good company, we have some good laughs at the Irish people."

The Tunnel, Glengarriff, Co. Cork.

© John Hinde Ireland Ltd.

Above: From the Adrian Healy collection, a John Hinde card of Glengarriff's so-called 'Blue Pool', which is a little inlet of Bantry Bay. This postcard was never posted.

Below: A Valentine's postcard of the Harold Peto-designed gardens on 'Garnish Island.' Ilnacullin (or 'Garnish Island' as it is more popularly known) is a small island in Bantry Bay, near Glengarriff, on which Harold Peto (1854-1933) designed and developed a series gardens for its owner John Annan Bryce (1874-1924), a native of Belfast, who, with his wife Violet, purchased the island from the British War Office in 1910. The gardens flourish in the mild humid micro-climate of the Gulf Stream-warmed Glengarriff harbour, and features among its many attractions a colonnaded Italian Garden, a Clock Tower, a Grecian Temple, and extensive woodland walkways with South American, Japanese, and many other plantations exotic in the Irish landscape. Violet Bryce died in 1939 and her son Roland bequeathed the island to the Irish nation in the 1950s. It is now administered and maintained by the Irish Heritage Service. This postcard, which is from the John James collection, was never posted.

GARNISH ISLAND AND MOUNTAINS, GLENGARRIFF.

A1857

PAT. O'SHEA Irish Bog Oak Dealer and his Sale Stall at Glengarriff, Co. Cork.

Two cards from the John James collection – **above** – a Fergus O'Connor card showing a Glengarriff street-side stall-holder selling bog-oak trinkets and walking sticks and postcards (bog oak: bits of ancient oak trees which have been preserved in bog-land soil, dramatically gnarled pieces – like sculptures by nature – which are polished and oiled and then packaged or mounted for presentation and sale). **Below:** A Lawrence card showing the Eccles Hotel near Glengarriff whose guestbook pages feature the names of many of the famous and celebrated – George Bernard Shaw, William Butler Yeats, etc. This postcard was never posted.

THE GLEN HOTEL Glengarriff, Co. Cork.

From the Adrian Healy collection, a Fergus O'Connor postcard of the Glen Hotel, Glengarriff. This postcard was never posted

© John Hinde Ireland Ltd.

Above: From the Adrian Healy collection, a John Hinde card showing Bantry town and beyond Bantry Bay (with part of Whiddy Island). This postcard was posted in Schull in the 1980s – judging by the stamp (it is not possible to make out the date of the post office cancellation mark) – but all it says in the address section is "Mr Dan Murphy": "Dear Dan and Pamela", the message begins, "We got down here safely. The weather is very good. Jack and Catherine are staying a short distance from us. Con is not too bad. Con was asking for your Patrick and Andy. From Maurine."

Below: From the Adrian Healy collection, a Lawrence card showing Bantry town with the town square at its centre. This card was posted in Bantry in May 1906, to a Miss Tindall at 10 Parliament Street in Harrogate, the brief message reads: "We are going on to Cork now."

Bantry Co. Cork.

IT SEEMS to rain a lot in Bantry. It had rained heavily the last time I had visited the town to see the official opening of the oil terminal at Whiddy Island, a much publicized event. BANTRY IS WAITING, the headline in the *Southern Star* had proclaimed. A new coating of tarmac was laid on the pier, and lines of trees appeared overnight. "The quickest wood I've ever seen grown."

The oil company also decorated the lamp posts with blue pennants and provided the lines of black Austin Princesses and Mercedes with orange stickers marked Gulf Oil. Tubs of flowers were placed in the old horse-trough in the main square, and crackly music was relayed through loudspeakers, which St Brendan the Navigator could not hear because he had a hood pulled over his head which would not be removed until the following day. He was another gift to the town from the company.

There had been an unusual air of festivity, as the presence of the P. & O. liner, *Orsova*, with the Taoiseach and other important guests aboard, livened up Bantry's usual deadly gloom. Except that it rained. Garda reinforcements patrolling the streets put on their waterproof capes. As the first guests disembarked from the ferry, they were pelted with a heavy shower while attendants rushed forward with armfuls of umbrellas. Mr Lynch and his party, the senior officials of Gulf Oil and their party, stood under the downpour making lengthy speeches until at last the statue of St Brendan was unveiled. He stood in a tiny boat with arms upraised, two monkish companions crouching behind him.

"She's a bit awkward with all them crowed together in the stern!"

Heads bent, the dignitaries departed rapidly to a banquet on board the *Orsova*, and soon the square was empty except for two lorries marked CHIPS and a queue of schoolgirls from the nearby convent buying ninepenny bags.

In the pubs men were remarking that the festivities must have cost a lot of money. "Sure it's nothing to that lot. They make a million on each ship – that's a million pounds to invest."

Gulf Oil had chosen Bantry for its new oil terminal after an exhaustive search around the coasts of Europe. It was the first large company to realize the advantages that the Bay afforded: a deep safe harbour and a government bending over backwards to entice it to settle in this depressed part of West Cork.

The company was tactful and generous, exhibiting an understanding of the dangers of polluting and disfiguring one of the best known tourist areas in Ireland. 'Gulf is Oil and an Attitude towards Mountains', ran its advertisements, published in many newspapers. "We are fully conscious of the wonderful scenery here," Mr E. D. Broderick, the chairman of Gulf had said. "It is our intention to preserve as fully as possible, while still accomplishing the purpose of our project." An artificial hill was raised to screen the unsightly lines of tanks like overblown mushrooms, and the tankers themselves, whose size appears to cleave the Bay in two.

From **The Coast of West Cork** *(Victor Gollancz, 1972), by Peter Somerville-Large.*

BANTRY, CO. CORK

© John Hinde Ireland Ltd.

From the Adrian Healy collection, a John Hinde card showing the square in Bantry and the statue of St Brendan the Navigator (presented to the town by Gulf Oil in the 1960s – see the extract from *The Coast of West Cork* on the page facing). This postcard has never been posted.

From the Adrian Healy collection, a postcard showing a Fair Day in the square in Bantry looking out towards Bantry Bay. The card has no publisher statement; it was posted in Bantry in December 1932, to a Miss Janet Knight at Prestwood, Great Missenden, Buckinghamshire, in England: "Dear Petkin," it begins, "Please thank Mummy very much for her P.C. and tell her I will write a nice long letter during the weekend. I hope that you are having a lovely time and being a good pet. I am looking forward to seeing you again soon, it seems such a long time since I left. Lots of love & kisses from Daddie. I wonder what you would like Father Xmas to give you or put in your stocking."

From the John James collection, a Lawrence postcard showing Bantry House (home of the earls of Bantry) and part of the head of Bantry Bay and Whiddy Island. This postcard was never posted.

From the Adrian Healy collection, a Lawrence card showing St Brendan's Church of Ireland church on the Square in Bantry. This card was posted in Bantry in 1908 – no written message – it is simply addressed: "Miss Rice | Hazelmere | 6, Kingston Cresent | Portsmouth | England" and in one corner of the card are what appear to be the initials "JS."

The Church Bantry Co.Cork.

VICKERY'S HOTEL, BANT

From the John James collection, a postcard of Vickery's Hotel, New Street, Bantry. This card was never posted and there is no publisher statement. On Vickery's Hotel, see facing page for commercial notice (advertisement) from *Stratten's Dublin, Cork, and South of Ireland* (1892).

© John Hinde Irreland Ltd.

BANTRY HOUSE, CO. CORK

From the Adrian Healy collection, a John Hinde postcard of Bantry House. This card has never been posted. On the B-side John Hinde has the following note on Bantry House: "Bantry House is set in magnificent surroundings and has a splendid collection of art treasures. Built around 1750, the house was formerly the home of the earls of Bantry, from whom the present owner is descended. The 2nd earl of Bantry added the south front to the house in 1840 and fitted it with a collection of tapestries and other works of art gathered during his travels in various parts of Europe."

VICKERY'S HOTEL, BANTRY
PROPRIETOR: MR GEORGE VICKERY

VISITORS to the lovely district of which Bantry forms the centre can find no better accommodation in the South of Ireland than that which obtains at that well-known establishment, VICKERY'S HOTEL, which has for so many years past opened wide its hospitable doors to the tourist and the traveller from all parts of the world. The history of this popular house dates back to 1855, when it was first opened by the father of the present proprietor, Mr George Vickery, who has, since the death of the founder in 1883, conducted the business with ever-increasing success. The Hotel premises are conveniently situated within one minute's walk of Bantry Bay, and close to the railway station, the building forming a handsome three-storied block, of which the new wing was added a few years ago to provide accommodation for the large increase of season visitors and tourists. The establishment is designed throughout on modern principles, the general arrangements and style of furnishing being of a very superior order, the apartments including spacious coffee, dining, and public drawing-room, large smoking-room, and fine commercial room for the exclusive use of commercial gentlemen. The bedrooms (twenty-five in number) are airy and comfortably furnished apartments. Special attention is directed to the most scrupulous cleanliness, and visitors may indulge in the luxury of hot and cold, plunge and spray baths, which have been fitted at considerable cost with all the newest improvements. The cooking and attendance are all that the most fastidious guest could desire, and the wine cellars of the establishment contain the choicest wines and spirits of the finest brands and of acknowledged excellence. In connection with the hotel is the largest posting establishment in the South of Ireland, all the public cars, coaches, and brakes running to Glengariff, *en route* for the famous Lakes of Killarney, being horsed by Mr Vickery, requiring a stud of from seventy-five to one hundred horses. For these, stabling accommodation for twenty-five is provided at Bantry, and there are additional stables at Glengariff, Kenmare, and Killarney, where the horses are changed. Mr Vickery also provides at the shortest notice cars and carriages with steady and reliable drivers for visitors desirous of exploring the objects of interest in the district, and an omnibus from the Hotel, bearing the name VICKERY'S HOTEL in large letters, attends the arrival of all trains. An efficient staff of well-trained servants is employed to wait upon the requirements of visitors to the Hotel, the whole arrangements of the management being capably conducted under the careful supervision of the genial proprietor, whose attentive consideration for the comfort of his guests has secured for him a wide measure of personal popularity and esteem from all who have at any time made VICKERY'S their headquarters while visiting the district.

Advertisement from **Stratten's Dublin, Cork, and South of Ireland** *(1892).*

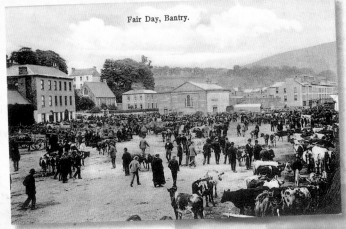

Fair Day, Bantry.

From the John James collection, this postcard of a Fair Day in Bantry was published by W. Vickery of Bantry. The postcard was never posted.

BANTRY CO. CORK

From the Adrian Healy collection, this 'Real Photo by Mason' postcard shows the railway terminal at Bantry, the end of the line for the West Cork railway service (a service that was decommissioned and dismatled in the early 1960s). The postcard was sent to a Mrs McNeight at 163 Herberton Road, Rialto, in Dublin: "Heard yesterday from Claire", the writer begins, "Am wondering how things will go when I get back. Meantime I'm enjoying here very much. Drive to Kenmare and Parknasilla was beautiful. Hope you, Ted & David are quite well. Until I see you | Love from CD."

GENERAL VIEW OF TOWN (BANTRY)

From the John James collection, a Philco Series postcard offering a view of Bantry town from the shoreline of Bantry Bay. This postcard was never posted.

DURRUS.

Dear

I am making many friends. Some stick tight already. Well — — —

From the Adrian Healy collection, a Birn Bros postcard from the "Stile Series" (Birn Bros., Ltd, Bunhill Row, London – trademark "B.B."). This card was posted in Durrus – a little village near Bantry – in 1910, to a Mr Joe Sullivan, Woollen Hall, Bantry (the B-side of the card is damaged and so not all of the message is legible): " <<*Illegible*>> your P.C. <<*Illegible*>> weeks ago. <<*Illegible*>> have <<*illegible*>> very much [for same]. So sorry I couldn't go to Bantry that Sat as I had a bad cold. Hope you enjoyed yourself ???? When <<*illegible*>> y[ou] <<*illegible*>> F.P. <<*Illegible*>> please drop an occasional P.C."

Facing page: From the John James collection, a "Signal Series" postcard (a trademark of E. & S. Ltd Publishers of Dublin and Belfast) showing Clover Hole, a highly regarded Bandon River fishing pool near Manch, east of Dunmanway – Kilcascan is a castillated house on the riverbank nearby. (The Bandon River rises in Mount Owen, north of Drimoleague, flows eastwards past Dunmanway, and through Ballineen, Enniskeane, Bandon, Innishannon, and then flows into the sea at Kinsale – see the extract from George Bennett's *History of Bandon*, pp. 119-20.) This postcard was posted in Ballineen (it looks like), however, stamp-hunters have removed the stamp and with it all of the information provided by the post office cancellation mark. The card was posted to a Mrs Shaw at 17 Lypiatt Terrace in Cheltenham, Gloucestershire in England (the handwriting is very poor): "Yes, have all kinds <<*cannot make out two words*>> Shall be so glad to have you again, M. O'Keefe."

From the John James collection, a Drimoleague Christmas postcard which is unstamped but written out for a Miss M.J. Dillon | Square | Bantry: "How are you getting on with our chef. What about the scarf, did you get thread for it. If weather permits Beckie and children will visit you next week. Tell Mr Patterson keep answers for [me?] Fondest love from your dearest cousin <<*cannot make out two words*>> the least forgetting <<*cannot make out one word*>> M.M.C."

From the Adrian Healy collection, a Frank Thomas Peyton postcard (using a Lawrence photograph) showing part of the Coom Valley near Dunmanway town. This postcard was never posted.

Coom Valley, Dunmanway, Co. Cork.

River Bandon, at Kilcascan, Clover Hole.

THE RIVER, as we have before said, rises in Mount Owen; and, rushing down its rugged sides, hides her young face among the water-lilies of Cullinaugh. Lingering there awhile, as if to catch a last look, or to bid eternal farewell to her mother mountain, she sets out on her long journey to the sea. Struggling through the thick sedge and the tall stout grass which besets her path, she hurries over a stony bed, skipping from boulder to boulder and from rock to rock, until she comes to the castle of the Togher. Loitering there awhile, on the skirt of the grassy lawn which oft felt the pressure of the foot of the thrice hospitable Teige O'Downy, and where her smooth waters oft mirrored the stalwart figure of that great mountain chief, she tardily moves along until she reaches the flat ground on which Dunmanway stands. The Kaal and another wide stream await her here, and pour their tributary waters into her fair bosom. Strengthened by these additions she proceeds; passing the walls of the dismantled keep where Randal Oge Hurly bid defiance to the Saxon, and sweeping by the sombre groves of Kilcaskin and the pine-covered hills of Manch, she arrives at Carrigmore. Here the Duvawain, springing from the classic region of "the steeple," and roaring down one of the rough valleys of Kennagh, co-mingles her dark waters with its own. Leaving Ballineen and Enniskeane behind her, she noiselessly approaches the ivy-clad trees and the time-worn front of "sweet Palace Anne."

From Palace Anne she flows on, past modest little country churches – past parsonages-county seats – past fields of corn – past grassy plains, echoing with the bleat of sheep and the low of cattle, until she tarries beneath the bridge at Carhue. Standing on the crest of an adjoining hill, and looking as far to the west as towering Sheehy and the lofty mountains of Dunmanway will permit, our beautiful river may be seen gleaming in the sun like a belt of burnished silver, as she slowly winds her way with graceful ease over a carpet of the brightest green. From Carhue to the town on which she has bestowed her name, "the pleasant Bandon" is once more among fair woods. Her course now lies through a wide valley, where huge oaks stretch out their gigantic arms, and fling broad shadows over many an acre of velvet turf; probably some of those oaks which the tourist, who visited this place when Elizabeth was still Queen of England, describes as trees of wonderful length. Herds of deer here bask on her verdant banks; and the waving willow dips the tips of its green tresses in her limpid stream. Flowing past that stately pile whose castellated walls enclose the site of the rude rath where St Fin Bar was born, she comes to Bandon. Refreshed by the waters of the Bridewell river, she again proceeds; and gliding by the riven walls of the mansion where Spenser's daughter dwelt, she flows into a wooden vale, and meets the Mugin at the Castle of Downdanial. Speeding past the ivyed bridge that spans that river's mouth and touching the very feet of the old fortalice of Barry Oge, she sweeps down between high hills draped to their very summit with the foliage of the oak and the beech; and entering a deeply-timbered dell, where tall dark trees spread gloom on her waters, she hurries again into the light, and, bending low, kisses the wavelets which the old ocean hath sent up to welcome her to its home.

From George Bennett's **History of Bandon, and of the principal towns in the West Riding of County Cork** *(1869).*

Chapel Lake, Dunmanway, Co. Cork.

E. C. Dawson, Publisher, Bandon, Co. Cork.   Guy's Autotypes.

From the Adrian Healy collection, a postcard published by E. C. Dawson of Bandon showing a party boating on Chapel Lake in Dunmanway. This card was never posted.

Sackville Street, Dunmanway, Co. Cork.

From the John James collection, a postcard published by Thomas Peyton of Dunmanway (using a Lawrence photo) showing Sackville Street in Dunmanway. The card was posted in Dunmanway in July 1914, to Mr & Mrs Wm Hill, 34 Gloucester Street, Eastville, Bristol, England: "July 7th | Dear Friends | We are now in Dunmanway visiting our Father's old home with his nephews and having a good time & feeling well. Hoping you are all well, Sincerely, M. Barry H Sheridan."

Carbery House, Dunmanway, Co. Cork.

Also from the John James collection, another Peyton-published postcard (again using a Lawrence photo) showing Carbery House in Dunmanway (Peytons had a drapery shop in Dunmanway). Carbery House was originally a Jacobean house (that is, the original structure dates from the 1680s), built by a rector of the Anglican parish of St Mary's. In the early 1900s – around the time this picture was made (this is the view of the house from the back garden) – it was the home of Mr Francis Fitzmaurice, a lawyer. This postcard was posted in Dunmanway (it looks like), however, stamp-hunters have removed the stamp and with it all of the information provided by the post office cancellation mark. The card was posted to a Miss D. Knight, Killinear, Enniskeane, Co. Cork: "This is a recent photo of our house. Do you recognise me? Mother is to be seen on the veranda if you look close enough. Many thanks for your P.C. I was delighted with it!! Isn't the weather awful? My love to Cara & self | Kindest regards from the family | Yours affec | Daisy F. | My dress was not blue nor my blouse pink!!!"

From the Adrian Healy collection, a John Hinde card offering a composite of images of Dunmanway town and its surrounding district. This postcard was never posted. On the reverse is the following John Hinde note on Dunmanway: "Situated in the heart of West Cork in the foothills of Sheehy Mountain, Dunmanway is a thriving market town and is an ideal place for touring West Cork which enjoys some of the finest scenery in Ireland."

DUNMANWAY, CO. CORK

AS YOU ENTER Dunmanway, you pass a sign saying: 'Best Kept Village 1982.' There's no mention of what's happened since.

The town is essentially a busy little square where three roads meet. The fairs my uncle used to bring me to, when hundreds of farmers used to pack the streets and pubs, are distant history. These days you'll see the West Cork company car – a tractor – parked up among the Toyotas and VWs, while its dishevelled bachelor farmer owner buys frozen meat and tinned vegetables in the supermarket, but that's progress for you.

Like many West Cork towns, Dunmanway was developed in the seventeenth century as a plantation, or settlement, by the English; records show that, by 1700, thirty English families were living there. In recent years the town has once again been settled by the English: not the well-heeled yachties you find in nearby Kinsale, Glandore, and Schull, but by alleged Crusties, hippies, druggies, pagans and New-Age travellers. In both cases, you could say that an English politician was responsible for the influx: first Oliver Cromwell, and then Margaret Thatcher, whose gimlet-eyed disapproval, and riot police, caused many unconventional young Brits to take their troublesome lifestyles across the Irish Sea. This must have pleased her no end.

From Pete McCarthy's **McCarthy's Bar: a journey of discovery in Ireland** *(Hodder and Soughton, 2000).*

From the John James collection, a postcard published by Frank Thomas Peyton of Dunmanway (using a Lawrence photo) showing St Mary's, the Anglican church in Dunmanway. Stamp-hunters have removed the stamp from this card and with it all of the information provided by the post office cancellation mark. The card was posted to a Mrs Matchelle, Ballintoy Rectory, Ballycastle, Co. Antrim: "Tuesday | Had a wire from Willie. He passed exam on Sat & yesterday. Lizzie."

From the Adrian Healy collection, a Lawrence postcard showing the Square in Dunmanway on a Fair Day. This postcard was never posted.

From the Adrian Healy collection, a Frank Thomas Peyton postcard (using a Lawrence photograph) showing Bridge Street, Dunmanway, on Fair Day.

BALLYBOY FAIR DAY IN DUNMANWAY.

From the Adrian Healy collection, a Cardall postcard showing horse racing and field events at the annual Ballabuidhe Horse Fair, which is a three-day horse-centred festival staged each year on the August Bank Holiday Weekend. Ballabuidhe – or, phonetically, 'Ballabwee' – is the ancient name for the area which is now Dunmanway, anglicized on this postcard to 'Ballyboy.' This card was never posted.

Residence of the late Colonel Shuldham, Coolkelure, Dunmanway, Co. Cork.

From the John James collection, a postcard showing Coolkelure House, northwest of Dunmanway, the residence of Colonel Harry Shuldham. As well as being signigicant West Cork landlords, the Shuldhams were a military family down through many generations – according to *Griffith's Valuations,* in the latter half of the 19th century, altogether the Shuldhams had 13,000 acres of land in Ireland. There is no publisher statement for this postcard; the photograph copyright is identified as that of 'W. Jagoe, Dunmanway.' The card was posted in Dunmanway in 1905, to a Master Hugh Mitchell at Mill House, Doneraile [Co. Cork]: "Wishing you a happy Christmas and New Year."

From the Adrian Healy collection, a Frank Thomas Peyton postcard showing St Mary's Convent School in Dunmanway. This postcard was never posted.

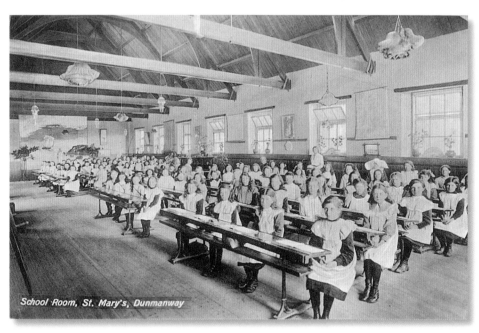

From the John James collection, a Lofthouse, Crosbie & Company postcard of St. Mary's Convent School, Dunmanway. This postcard was posted in November 1932, to Messers Lalor Ltd, Cook Street, Cork: "St Mary's | Dunmanway | Co. Cork | 7th Nov. 1932 | Please send card with diameter measurements for Mass and Benediction candles & oblige | Sisters of Charity." Lalor Church Candles Limited was a candle manufactory at 12 Cook Street, Cork.

At Inchigeela Co. Cork.

This postcard showing cows watering in the River Lee at Inchigeela is from the Adrian Healy collection. There is no publisher statement and the postcard was never posted (however, in the stamp-box it says that a halfpenny stamp must be affixed, therefore the card appears to be from the early 1900s).

Inchigeela Co. Cork.

From the John James collection, this Lawrence picture postcard of haymaking at Inchigeela was never posted.

THE NORTH COUNTRY

33 MILES northwest of Cork – 11 miles from Macroom and 24 from Bantry – Inchigeela possesses both Protestant and Catholic churches, a sub post-office, a constabulary station, two schoolhouses, an hotel, etc. The surface is mountainous, rocky and of wild aspect, but towards the east more level, and in a profitable stage of cultivation. About ten miles west of the village is the romantic "lone" lake of Gougane Barra – the source of the Lee. This lake is situated in a picturesque and sequestered spot, in a lofty chain of mountains between Cork and Kerry, the utter loneliness and stern magnificence of which it is difficult to conceive; and in whose rugged and precipitous acclivities the golden eagle is said still to breed. St Finbarr – who founded a large school or monastery, towards the end of the sixth century, around which the city of Cork developed – lived for some time as a hermit in a cell on a small islet in the lake. A long series of ascetics succeeded him here, the last of whom was named O'Mahony, who lived in this lonely spot for twenty eight years and died in 1700. This small island… is overshadowed by venerable ash trees. It is connected with the shore by a rude artificial causeway, and the greater portion of its surface is covered by the ruins of a chapel, and a cloister containing eight cells, rudely constructed of brown stone. Close to the mountains encircling Gougane Barra is the celebrated Pass of Keimaneigh (the path of the deer), through which runs the high road between Macroom and Bantry. The mountain has been divided by some convulsion of nature: precipitous walls of rock, clothed in wild ivy, ferns and mosses, rise to a height of several hundred feet on either side of the gorge. Between the lake of Gougane and Inchigeela the Lee expands into a broad sheet of water, called Lough Allua, the eastern extremity of which is about a mile from Inchigeela. The lake (or rather series of lakes) is about four miles in length by one in breadth. All the adjacent country is called Iveleary, from the sept of the O'Learys, its ancient owners, and to whom also belonged the castles of Carrignacurra (Castle-Masters) and Dromcarra, on the Lee towards Macroom. Carrignacurra was garrisoned by Cromwell's troops, and is still in tolerable preservation, consisting of a square tower about 100 feet high. About two centuries ago this locality now almost entirely destitute of timber, was a vast forest of oak, birch, ash, and yew, abounding with red and fallow deer. There are vast marshes here, clothed with heather and aquatic plants, and in their seasons, frequented by great quantities of water fowl. Attempts, hitherto abortive, have been made to drain this extensive quagmire. Formerly, some metallic cubes, yellow and shining like gold, were found in this district, and metallic ores have, from time to time, been washed out of the adjacent rocks during floods. About midway between Inchigeela and Gougane is the village of Ballingeary, with a Catholic church and National schools.

From **Guy's Postal Directory of Cork** *(1886).*

Facing page: From the John James collection, detail from a Lawrence postcard showing the village of Inchigeela near Macroom. This postcard was never posted.

Inchigeela Lakes between Inchigeela and Ballingeary, West Cork, Ireland

Colour Photo by John Hinde, F.R.P.S.

© John Hinde Ireland Ltd.

From the Adrian Healy collection, a John Hinde postcard showing a view of the lake lands near Inchigeela. This postcard was never posted.

Lake Hotel Inchigeela Co Cork.

A Lawrence postcard from the John James collection showing the Lake Hotel at Inchigeela with, in the foreground, a summer touring party. This postcard was never posted.

ON THURSDAY, July 21st we rested all day and next day we boarded a bus at 6.30 p.m. that took us to my native village of Inchigeela...

Well, here I was at last steering westward to fulfil a desire existing in my heart for a long time. A hope, yes, a cherished hope – I often thought in vain – was now at last to come true...

When we got to within five miles of the village I started to look out for familiar places and scenes. Yes, here was Toonsbridge. I wonder who has the public house now. Dan Dineen's farm on the left. The hill of Milleen. Herlihys lived here on the right. Oh, oh, Dan the Loggs house was torn down! Rossmore hill doesn't seem so steep anymore and on reaching the top I can see the village.

Oh, hAnam an Diabhal, there it is! There it is "my native Inchigeel, near the town of sweet Macroom." From now on I expect the ghosts of my ancestors will be greeting me. As I am passing Joss Kelleher's I can hear him singing in his fine rich voice, "Mo vesteen leigh", although I know he is gone to the great beyond these many years.

Here we are at the hotel. I am greeted first by Timmie Johnny O'Sullivan, proprietor of the hotel and a former schoolmate of mine. His wife too welcomes me and Neilus Kelleher ex-postman comes sauntering in to bid me a "cead mile failte." A member of the Garda Siochana and Paddy Casey drop in later and we sit and talk late into the night. We are then shown to our room and prepare to retire. But I had a great desire to satisfy an impulse: as a boy I always thought I would like to stand inside this hotel and look out, instead of standing outside looking in. I now was in a position to satisfy this desire so I strolled over to the window, raised the shade and looked outside.

I did not believe my eyes! I rubbed my optics as I thought I was observing an optical illusion or maybe 'twas all a dream. This could not be true. Maybe my whole trip to Ireland was a dream and I'll wake up in Peabody. I pinch myself. No, it is not a dream: here was my wife in the room with me. There is Delae's Hotel across the street (now Creedon's). There is Quinlan's house and Thade Aherne's, and Johnny Barry's and the Post Office where I worked. No, it cannot be a dream. If anybody told me they saw the streets of my native Inchigeela lit up with electric lights I would not believe them. I wonder is it because I'm returned that they are lighting the place up? I run down stairs and inquire as to what was the cause for the illumination. They tell me the village has been lit up for these six months past now.

*From 'An Exile's Rambles through Erin', by Jerh O'Riordan (**Ballingeary & Inchigeela Historical Society Journal**, 2000).*

Holy Island Gougane Barra Co. Cork.

From the John James collection, a Lawrence card showing Holy Island in the lake at Gougane Barra. This postcard was posted in Macroom in August 1910 to H. Smith Esq., 99 Patrick Street, Cork: "I just got your note", the sender writes, "I told Mr Roberts to send only 2 lbs of butter while we are away as the maids are in the house, please send it to Tivoli on Saturdays. It does not matter about last Saturday's, E. Levis."

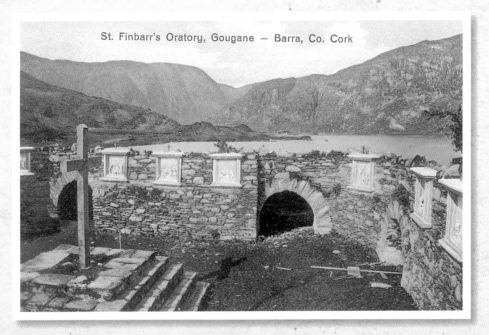

St. Finbarr's Oratory, Gougane — Barra, Co. Cork

Another Lawrence card of Gougane Barra from the John James collection, this one showing part of the ruins of St Finbarr's Oratory on Holy Island (a nineteenth century rebuild/reconstruction of an older oratory). This postcard was never posted.

GOUGANE BARRA

WEST CORK

From the Adrian Healy collection, a Real Ireland postcard showing St Finbarr's Oratory on Holy Island, Gougane Barra. This building was built in the early 1900s (1902) and stands beside the ruins of an older oratory – pictured in the second of the postcards on the page facing – which itself is a nineteenth century rebuild commemorating an even older oratory (all of which commemorate the original oratory on this site which was St Finbarr's in the sixth century).

From the Adrian Healy collection, a postcard of Cúil Aodha ('Coolea' is its anglicized form), the picture part of which is an oil-on-canvas painting by Maire Ni Shuilleabhain; postcard published by Maire Ni Shuilleabhain's studio – Studio Eas Coille, Baile Mhuirne, Co. Cork. Cúil Aodha/Coolea is up in the mountains between Ballingeary

Cúil Aodha

and, further north, Ballyvourney (Ballyvourney in Gaelic is 'Baile Mhuirne' – Cúil Aodha and Baile Mhuirne are Gaeltacht or Ghaeltacht areas, which is to say territories that are predominately Irish-speaking). This postcard has not been posted, however, on the reverse are the following notes: "'Mo Scéal Féin' | An tAthair Peadar O'Laoire. | 'Séadhna' (Seana)." And in another hand "Sean O'Riada (Reidy) | Sean Dunne | Sean O'Riordán (poets)." *Mo Scéal Féin* (1915) – My Own Story – is a memoir by Peadar Ua Laoghaire (1839-1920) – Peter O'Leary – a Catholic priest, writer, Gaelic scholar, and in the late nineteenth century and early twentieth one of the leading figures in the effort to save the remnants of the Gaelic language and culture. Sean O'Riada (1931-71) is a composer and poet who lived and worked in Cúil Aodha/Coolea (Reidy is the anglicized form of O'Riada). Sean Dunne (1956-95) was a writer and poet. And Sean O'Riordán (1916-77) was also a poet, an Irish language poet. All are closely connected to the Cúil Aodha/Coolea and Baile Mhuirne/Ballyvourney areas and to the Gaelic Revival movement.

From the John James collection, a Lawrence postcard of Ballingeary, a village midway between Inchigeela and Gougane Barra. This postcard was posted in 1935 to a Miss H. Butterfield at Rathsallagh, Colbinstown, Co. Wicklow: "Having a great time here. We got a spin to Glengarriff the other day. It is a beautiful place. Love to all, Fanny."

A Lawrence postcard from the Adrian Healy collection showing the bridge over the Sullane River in Macroom and, in the background, Macroom Castle. The postcard was never posted – however, in the stamp box it says that a halfpenny stamp must be affixed, therefore the card appears to be from the early 1900s.

THE TOWN HALL AND SQUARE, MACROOM, CO. CORK

From the John James collection, a Cardall Series card showing the Town Hall in Market Square in Macroom. This postcard was posted in what was probably the 1980s, sent to RTE (the national television and radio broadcasting service in Ireland) in response to a competition – Wedding Comp, PO Box No 2712, Live at 3, Donnybrook, Dublin 4: "For Derdie Hartnett & Don O'Leary" the message part begins; it continues "1. Fred Astaire | 2. Emmet Bergin | 3. Humphrey Bogart." Fred Astaire and Humphrey Bogart are mid-twentieth century Hollywood film actors and Emmet Bergin is an Irish film, television, and stage actor. At the bottom of the message part of the card the sender has put her name and address: "Mrs Peggy McCarthy, Clonmoyle, Kilmichael, Macroom, Co. Cork."

© John Hinde Ireland Ltd.

MACROOM CASTLE, CO. CORK

From the Adrian Healy collection, a John Hinde postcard of the entryway to the grounds of Macroom Castle from the town square. On the B-side of the card the John Hinde company has the following note: 'Macroom is an important marketing centre in the picturesque valley of the Sullane River. The castle in the town was the scene of many a siege, particularly in the 16th and 17th centuries. The castle and town of Macroom were at one time the property of Admiral Sir William Penn, whose son founded the state of Pennsylvania.' This postcard was never posted.

This postcard of Macroom Castle, from the John James collection, was published by a 'Miss Mescal, Macroom.' It was never posted. Having been burned out during the War of Independence (1919-22) eventually Macroom Castle was demolished altogether (for safety sake) in the 1960s. It is thought that it was originally built (as a castle) by the Carew Clan in the reign of King John (1199-1216), on the site of an earlier stronghold. Afterwards it passed into the hands of the MacCarthy Clan when they became overlords in the territory. In 1650 Bishop Boetius McEgan failed to hold it for the MacCarthys against Cromwellian forces, as a result of which McEgan was taken and hanged at Carrigadrohid.

Afterwards, the castle was granted, as a reward, to Sir William Penn (father of William Penn of Pennsylvania) who lived there for some time before selling it on to the Hollow Sword Blade Company, a property-speculating investment house in London. Macroom Castle eventually became part of the property portifolio of the Bernards of Bandon.

Roman Catholic Church, Macroom.   616/9

From the John James collection, a Macroom Printing Works postcard of St Colman's, the Roman Catholic church in Macroom. Built in the 1820s, St Colmans is a Thomas Deane building (Thomas Deane, 1792-1871), the high altar by a young John Hogan (1800-58), a Deane *protégé*, a sculptor who switched from a legal career to apprentice in Deane's firm where his talents for drawing and carving were fostered. This postcard was never posted.

Macroom.

The River and Carrigadrohid Castle.

The Wrench Series, No. 9939

From the Adrian Healy collection, a postcard of Carrigadrohid Castle on the River Lee, near Macroom (6 miles east of Macroom), a Wrench Series postcard (No. 9939). This postcard was posted in Macroom on 20 August 1904, to a Miss Marion Hosford, c/o Mrs Griffith, 10 Porkington Terrace, Barmouth, in Wales, and is simply signed "Sydney." Carrigadrohid (which translates as 'the rock of the bridge' or 'bridge rock' – the castle is built on a rock island in the middle of the river, the bridge also using the rock island as one of its pillars) is another MacCarthy castle; it is not known exactly when the castle and bridge where built but documents establish that they were in place – and known as 'Carrigadrohid' – by the 1570s.

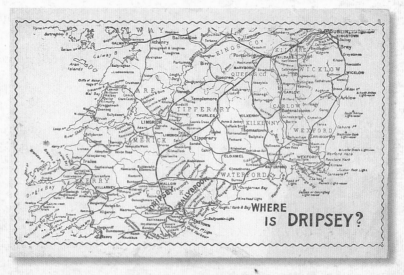

WHERE IS DRIPSEY?

From the John James collection, the 'Where is Dripsey?' card is a production of the Dripsey Woollen Mills company, a promotional device – one of a series. This postcard was never posted. Also on the River Lee – on a tributary of the River Lee, very near where it joins the senior flow – Dripsey is about 10 kilometres east of Carrigadrohid (and about 18 kilometres from Cork city).

From the John James collection, a Fergus O'Connor postcard of Dripsey Castle (sometimes also Carrignamuck Castle) – which is about 10 kilometres east of Carrigadrohid (and about 18 kilometres from Cork city). The B-side is unstamped, undated, and without a postal address, however the following message is written on it by a Mr W. Robinson: "Dear Walter, your dear father will be travelling along here on Saturday afternoon. You will observe that it is beautiful country. Your loving father, W. Robinson." On the banks of the Dripsey (in Gaelic 'Druipseach', meaning "muddy river"), a tributary of the River Lee, Dripsey

Dripsey Castle on the Lee.   Co. Cork.

Castle was built in the late 15th century, part of a chain of MacCarthys-of-Muskerry castles which ran from Blarney to west of Macroom (a chain of castles which also included those at Carrigadrohid and Macroom).

Kilcrea Abbey, Co. Cork

From the John James collection, a Valentine Series postcard of the ruins of Kilcrea Abbey. The card was posted in September 1911 to Miss J. Cloake at Bagmill Farm, Saltash in Cornwall in England: "Dear J", the message begins, "How would you like a nice country walk with Bert around here. From Alec." Kilcrea Abbey (also known as 'Kilcrea Friary') was built in the 1460s, a Franciscan foundation. It is located on the site of an earlier monastery, and named after Saint Cyra, whose remains are interred in the centre of the choir. Kilcrea was officially suppressed in the 1540s during the English Reformation but continued in use under MacCarthy patronage. It was sacked by English troops in 1580s during the suppression of the Desmond Rebellion. Nevertheless, on and off, monks continued to attempt to occupy the place for generations – even up until the beginning of 19th century. The little river in the picture is the River Bride, a tributary of the River Lee.

Tubrid Well, Millstreet, County Cork

Facing page: From the Adrian Healy collection, a Justborn Photography postcard of Millstreet's Tubrid Holy Well and Marion shrine. This postcard was never posted. 'In the month of May each year vast numbers of people young and old travel to the holy well of Tubrid near the town of Millstreet to "do the rounds." Their pagan ancestors came to worship the waters of that same well two thousand years ago. People come now to pray the rosary and drink the healing waters...' (text from Millstreet.ie, which is the Millstreet local area website, it continues) 'However, it is false to imagine that pilgrims doing rounds at holy wells are simply carrying on the old pagan tradition. Nor is the veneration of these holy wells a superstition. It is well to remember that prayers to the saints, in any spot hallowed by their abode, their miracles or their labours, are all the more likely to be efficacious and rewarded. At Tubrid, according to their faith and if it be the will of God, people are cured by the holy waters of the well. A cripple leaves a crutch for all to see and walks away. A girl has her hair restored by washing in the well, an eight-year old child begins to talk, a woman has her finger straightened, an American gets relief from arthritis, a priest has a speech-impediment cured. An invalid thirty years in bed gets up and walks again after she has donated the stones for the building of the Grotto. Such is the story of the well. Such is the faith of the people who come to the well. Such is the providential role of Mary, standing sentinel over the healing waters, drawing the people to herself so that she may guide them to the unfathomable riches of Our Lord's life, as seen through her eyes, and unfolded to them in the Mysteries of the Rosary.'

Kilmeedy Castle, Millstreet, County Cork

Above: From the Adrian Healy collection, a Justborn Photography postcard of Kilmeedy Castle near Millstreet. This postcard was never posted. 'Built in 1436 Kilmeedy Castle was never a residential place, it was a military stronghold, built to command the wild mountain pass between Cork and Kerry... The national flag is flown from the castle top on special occasions, such as the coming of the Pope to Ireland and the hosting of the Eurovision Song Contest in Millstreet' (from Millstreet.ie – the Eurovision Song Contest was staged in Millstreet in 1993, it was held at the Green Glens Arena, a large indoor equestrian centre just outside the town; Pope John Paul II visited Ireland in 1979).

Convent of the Holy Infant Jesus, Drishane, Millstreet.

From the Adrian Healy collection, a Lofthouse, Crosbie & Company postcard of the Convent of the Holy Infant Jesus at Drishane (on the history of Drishane, see extract on facing page). This postcard was posted in Millstreet, to a Miss J. Murray at Mount Pleasant House, Strokestown, County Rosscommon: "Drishane Convent, Millstreet, Co. Cork" the writer – Jennie Griffin – begins (her closely-written message), "Dearest Josephine – How are you and each dear one in Mount Pleasant. Give my love to Ida and also to your dear Dada & Mama. I returned to Drishane on the 14th. I was rather lonely at first but am quite happy now. This is an exquisite convent. I only wish you could visit it. This is only a side view of the convent. I will send you more views later. Dear Josephine I will ask you to do me a favour & that is to write often to me. I shall expect a long letter during the week. Goodbye & oceans of love to all from Jennie U. Griffin. Now be sure and write long letter when you get this. J.G. Give my love to dear Ida and ask her to write also. I shall send you 2 long letters next Sunday. J.G."

Drishane Bridge, Millstreet, Co Cork

This postcard of Drishane Bridge is from the Adrian Healy collection, published by the Lawrence company of Dublin. The card was never posted.

Drishane Castle, Millstreet, County Cork

From the Adrian Healy collection, a Justborn Photography postcard of Drishane Castle, Millstreet (on Drishane Castle, see extract from Millstreet.ie, below). This postcard was never posted.

THE LOVELY castle and grounds of Drishane are situated a little to the northeast of Millstreet, near where the Finnow River joins the great Blackwater flow.

The old tower-house, which was built by the MacCarthys in the 1400s, is in very fine condition.

MacCarthy lands were finally fully forfeited following the Jacobite-Williamite war of 1690 [William of Orange v. James II], and Drishane came into the possession of the Hollow Sword Blade Company, which had financed William's campaign in Ireland. In 1709 the estate was sold to Henry Wallis of Ballyduff, Co. Waterford.

…the Wallis family appear to have been popular in the neighbourhood and presided at Drishane until the 1880s when the estate was placed in Chancery on the application of a number of insurance companies, where it remained until 1912 when it was sold to Patrick Stack of Fermoy from whom, through the offices of Cornelius Duggan of Cork, it passed to the Dames of Saint Maud, a French order of teaching nuns (the Congregation of the Holy Infant Jesus). The Drishane Sisters remained until 1992 when the estate was purchased from them by Noel C. Duggan, a local businessman. Initially a hotel was envisaged. Then Kosovar refugees were quartered there during the post-Yugoslavia (Balkan) meltdown, following which it has continued as an accommodation facility for refugee peoples while their asylum applications are processed.

From the 'History' section of www.millstreet.ie

A postcard of the National School in Millstreet from the John James collection, published by the Lawrence company of Dublin. This postcard was never posted. The [British] Board of Education established the National School system of primary education in Ireland in the 19th century, rolling it out across the country from the mid-century onwards. It was designed to produce a workforce equipped to function in the industrial economy and in the reformed political system. Despite opposition from those who felt that the focus of an Irish education system ought to be the production of Irish Catholics – as opposed to British workers – the National School system prospered and by 1900 there were nearly 9,000 of them across the country, 753 in County Cork. The Victorian

National School system was criticised (and obstructed) because it did not, for example, offer religious instruction, or teach the Irish language, or Irish history. The school buildings were constructed after an architectural set of templates so that, from Bere Island to the Blackwater river valley, National Schools in every town and village looked more or less like the one pictured here in this Millstreet postcard.

Mill Race, Millstreet   Co. Cork

From the John James collection, a postcard of the Mill Race in Millstreet – the stream is called the 'Mill Race' – a card printed for J.J. O'Mahony of Millstreet; however, apparently, this is a Lawrence photograph from 1910, by Robert French (National Library of Ireland Catalogue, The Lawrence Photograph Collection). According to Guy's

Postal Directory for 1914, J.J. O'Mahony was a grocery shopkeeper and coal merchant in Millstreet. According to the same source O'Mahony also had a house-furniture and hardware enterprise, a boot and shoe shop as well as being listed as a purveyor of stationary supplies and china and glassware. This postcard was never posted.

PATRICK PEARSE [one of the leaders of the nationalist 'Easter Rising' of 1916] became the Irish Volunteers' Director of Military Organisation in 1914 and by 1915 he was on the IRB's Supreme Council [IRB: Irish Republican Brotherhood], and its secret Military Council, the core group that began planning for a Rising. In that role he visited Millstreet on 22 August 1915 to meet local IRB members and Volunteers. The following [from Jim Cronin's *Millstreet's Green and Gold*] provides a brief account of the visit:

"A Unit of the Irish Volunteers had been formed locally in 1914 after the disintegration of the National Volunteers. It was so pain-stakingly organised that it was considered by the Volunteer Executive in Dublin to be a suitable nucleus for organising the Duhallow and Muskerry districts. Accordingly, they sent Padraig Pearse to Millstreet to address a meeting of the public and a convention of Volunteers. Pearse's visit on August 22nd was ostensibly for the local Feis and sports [day]. The advertised programme read: 'Gaelic and Athletic events – Tug-o'-war, pony race, championship dancing, and address on the Resurrection of Erin, by P. H. Pearse, B.A., B.L.'

The organisers were: Tom Griffin and Seamus (Jimmy) Hickey. As the visit took place only a fortnight after his famous oration at the grave of O'Donovan Rossa it attracted a lot of attention, not least from the R.I.C. [Royal Irish Constabulary – the police force for the British authorities in Ireland]

However, Pearse slipped through them and made his way to the football field. There he addressed several thousand people who had assembled to enjoy a real Gaelic day and to listen to the gospel of Irish patriotism as preached by its greatest exponent of the time. His address reawakened in many the dormant spirit of Irish patriotism inherited from an unyielding and freedom loving ancestry. More than a few resolved to give their lives if necessary that Ireland might be free.

Amongst those present were Jeremiah O'Reardon and Jim Buckley, who had been active with the Fenians in 1867, and many veterans of the Land War of the 1880s. Others were mere boys [and young men] who had learned well the history of their native land.

Following a conference with Pearse, these men and others set to work to expand the organisation of the Volunteers. When the R.I.C. realised that Pearse had evaded them their chagrin was of a high order. However, they had the privilege of standing guard outside the Railway Hotel whilst Pearse had an evening meal inside. It is a significant fact that all those known to be associated with his visit were either interned or had to go on the run the following year.

A Millstreet Miscellany 3 [various authors], Aubane Historical Society, 2010. [All of the above is taken from *A Millstreet Miscellany 3*, most of which is an extract from Jim Cronin's *Millstreet's Green and Gold* (Millstreet GAA, 1984) – that is, only the first paragraph is by the Aubane Historical Society's editors, the producers of *A Millstreet Miscellany 3*. Matter in square brackets, however, is by the editor of the present volume.]

The Presbytery. Millstreet. Co Cork

A Lawrence postcard of the Millstreet presbytery from the Adrian Healy collection (a presbytery is the residence for Roman Catholic priests). This postcard was never posted.

R.C. Church, Millstreet. Co. Cork.

From the John James collection, a Lawrence card showing St Patrick's, the Roman Catholic church in Millstreet. This postcard was never posted. Commissioned and built in the 1830s, the architectural design of St Patrick's is attributed to the Pain brothers, English architects who designed many church buildings in Cork in the period, including the Catholic churches in Kinsale, Dunmanway, and Bantry, as well, of course, as their best-known work in Cork, the old courthouse on what is now Washington Street in Cork city (which burned down in the 1890s, only the pillared façade of the Pain brothers' courthouse building survives).

A postcard of Dhuarigle Castle from the John James collection, a Lawrence card – 'J.J. O'Mahony, Millstreet, Co. Cork' is also printed – not in the original print, printed subsequently (on J.J. O'Mahony, see the caption for Coole House, below). This postcard was never posted. Originally built as an O'Keeffe possession in the 16th century, following the revolutions and restorations of the turbulent 17th century Dhuraigle was in the hands of the Hollow Sword Blade Company, a London investment house that had financed the Prince William of Orange campaign in Ireland. By the 1720s, Dhuarigle belonged to Henry Maule, the Anglican bishop of Cloyne. It was leased and sub-leased many times after that, but by the 19th century it was the possession of Ellen Wallis, one of the Wallises of Drishane Castle, who in turn left it to her daughters. The building pictured is not, of course, the original castle, it is a rebuild, dating from *circa* 1810.

From the John James collection, a postcard of Coole House, Millstreet, a card published by J.J. O'Mahony of Millstreet; however, apparently, this is a Lawrence photograph from 1910, by Robert French (National Library of Ireland Catalogue, The Lawrence Photograph Collection). According to *Guy's Postal Directory* for 1914, J. J. O'Mahony was a shopkeeper (groceries) and coal merchant in Millstreet. According to the same source O'Mahony also had a house-furniture and hardware enterprise, a boot and shoe shop as well as being listed as a purveyor of stationary supplies and china and glassware. Built in the 1760s (*Burke's Guide to Irish Country Houses*), Coole House was the property of the O'Donnells – Herbert O'Donnell and his descendants – who were land agents for the Wallis family at Drishane Castle.

Ireland

Just north of Millstreet is the N72, the high road to Killarney – turn left to go west for Killarney, or go right to go east for Mallow and Mitchelstown or for the road to Cork city. If you cross the highway and go north you come to Newmarket. This Real Ireland postcard – which is from the Adrian Healy collection – has never been posted.

GOING TO SCHOOL and coming back was so enjoyable that it made school itself bearable. My main objection to school was that I had to stay there: it was the first experience to interfere with my freedom and it took a long time to accept that there was no way out of its trap. I could look out through a window in the back wall of the schoolhouse and see my home in the distance, with the fields stretching out invitingly and the Darigle river glinting in the valley. I made many an imaginary journey home through that window: it was not that I wished to be at home so much, but I wanted to be free to ramble through the fields. I envied the freedom of the crows in the trees, coming and going as they pleased.

But school became an accepted pattern eventually and even though it had its black days it had its good ones as well. The black days were mainly in winter when we arrived through the fields with sodden boots and had to sit in the freezing cold with a harsh wind whipping under the door and up through the floorboards. The school was an old stone building with tall rattling windows and black cobweb-draped rafters, and when the wind howled the whole school groaned and creaked. The floor had large gaping holes through which an occasional rat peeped up to join the educational circle…

The school had just two rooms. The master had a room to himself and the second room was shared by the two other teachers: one taught infants and first class at one side of the room, while second and third classes were taught by the second teacher at the other

From the Adrian Healy collection, a postcard of Newmarket with no publisher statement. This card was never posted.

side. It was open-plan education and if you got bored at your end you could tune in to the other side, at the risk of a slap across the ear if you were caught out.

We ate our lunch, which consisted of a bottle of milk and two slices of home-made brown bread, sitting on a grassy ditch running around the school, and we fed the crumbs to the birds. In winter the bottles of milk were heated around the fire during class-time, often resulting in corks popping from the heat, and if the top could not pop because it was screwed on we had a mini-explosion and a milk lake.

There was a cottage near the school from which we collected a pot of tea each day for the teachers, and this provided a welcome diversion, especially in summer. We went down a narrow lane which led into a long garden abounding with rows of vegetables, fruit trees, and flowers. These flowers overflowed onto the paths and climbed up over the windows and onto the thatched roof of the cottage: it was almost buried in flowers, and when you went down the steps and through the doorway you stepped into another world.

From **To School Through the Fields** *(Brandon, 1988), by Alice Taylor.*

From the John James collection, a postcard of the Newmarket Show, possibly 1914. There is no publisher statement for this card. On the B-side, in the stamp-box area, there is a date '1914.' This postcard was never posted. A Miss Margaret Murphy used the card to try out forms of her name and address: 'Miss Margaret Murphy' is written twice; 'Miss Margaret Murphy, Co. Cork' is written three times; 'Miss Margaret Murphy, Co. Cork, Ireland' is written three times; and finally the full form of her address is written out 'Miss Margaret Murphy, Newstreet West, Newmarket, Co. Cork, Ireland.' '1914' is in the same hand and in the same ink.

Also from the John James collection, another Newmarket Show postcard, from 1917, published by Guy & Co., Cork. This postcard was never posted.

THE COURT, NEWMARKET, CO. CORK.

From the John James collection, this postcard of Aldworth's Court just outside of Newmarket has never been posted. There is no publisher statement but the photography is, evidently, by Wilkie's of Cork (Wilkie & Son photographic studio, 48A King Street [now MacCurtain Street]; the business seems to have been established in the 1890s and was in operation until the 1940s). Newmarket Court was designed for the Aldworth family by Isaac Rothery in the mid-18th century (over Mallow way Rothery also designed Bowen's Court and Doneraile Court). The Aldworths came to Ireland in the 1600s and, by the end of the century, had established themselves in what became the locality of Newmarket. The family intermarried with the St Legers of Doneraile, the Rogers of Lota, and the Olivers of Castle Oliver, county Limerick, and other leading families in the region. The last of the Aldworths to live in Newmarket Court was Major John Charles Oliver Aldworth. He died in England in 1927. Newmarket Court was then purchased on behalf of the Sisters of St Joseph, who used it as a training centre for nuns destined for Australia. Afterwards, in the 1970s, the place was bought by Conor O'Flynn who sold it to the Newmarket Development Association under whose auspices it became the James O'Keeffe Memorial Institute. The institute is the headquarters for IRD Duhallow, which is a community-based integrated rural development company concerned with the economic and cultural life of Newmarket and the Duhallow territory (Duhallow is a barony, like Carbery, or Muskerry). The building functions as a Teagasc Training Centre, as well as providing administrative offices for small enterprise units, a food production incubator unit, and FÁS (Irish National Training and Employment Authority – Foras Áiseanna Saothaire) services, it also houses an agricultural museum and a local heritage centre.

Kanturk.
The Old Court.

12 April 1904.
For little Vivi's Book.
I hope Muriel's cold is very much
better. Love to all from Papa.

From the Adrian Healy collection, this Guy & Co. postcard of Kanturk Castle was posted on 12 April 1904, to a Miss Vivienne P. Morris at Aeta Place, St Lukes, Cork: "For little Vivi's Book. I hope Muriel's cold is very much better. Love to all from Papa." Kanturk Castle was a Tudor build for MacDonagh MacCarthy, lord of Duhallow, completed in the early 1600s. The name 'Kanturk' comes from the Gaelic 'Céann Tuirc' which means boar's head – and, indeed, the town's crest is a heart-shaped shield divided in two down the middle with representations of a boar's head (on a white background) on one side and Kanturk Castle on the other (on a green background).

KANTURK

This composite of Kanturk street-scenes is from the Adrian Healy collection. There is no explicit publisher statement but the photography is credited to M. & S. Scully. The postcard has never been posted.

This aerial view of Kanturk is from the John James collection, a card published by Aerofilms Ltd., Elstree Way, Boreham Wood, Hertfordshire, England. The postcard has never been posted. Kanturk is a town built around the confluence of the Allow and Dallow, tributaries to the great Blackwater, a river which is the principal feature of the geography and economy and culture of North Cork.

[THE OLYMPIC HERO] was met outside the town by a convey of cars, the convey including General O'Duffy, Chief Superintendent Clinton, and Superintendent O'Sullivan (Kanturk), who travelled in the same car as Dr O'Callaghan for the remainder of the journey.

At Curragh, a mile from the town, a large gathering had assembled, including the Cork Butter Exchange Brass and Reed Band. Amongst those who marched carrying banners were members of the Duhallow Camogie Club, Fianna Fáil, Kanturk GAA, Old Road Tug-o'-War teams, and Droumtarriffe Football Club. The procession paraded the different streets, after which a public meeting was held in the Square, presided over by the Right Rev. Monsignor Madigan, PP, VG, at which Dr O'Callaghan was presented with a beautiful illuminated address from the priests and people of Kanturk and district. The address was read by Rev. J. Roche, CC.

Replying, Dr O'Callaghan said that the reception extended to him by the people of Kanturk and Duhallow was the finest he had got. He counselled everybody to avoid

criticism and pull together. The future of the nation depended on the young people.

Rev. P. Brown, Rector, Kanturk, acting chairman of the reception committee, said it was an extraordinary thing to be a world champion, but to retain the title, as Dr O'Callaghan did at the Los Angeles Olympic Games, was a unique performance.

General O'Duffy said if it were not for Duhallow they would have no athletic revival movement.

The Rev. Father M. O'Mullane, a native of the district, who is on holidays from America, said they had the facilities in America for athletics, but they lacked the spirit of Ireland.

Mr Thomas Barry, hon. secretary of Duhallow Athletic Club, also spoke. A banquet, at which the Rev. Father John Roche presided, was subsequently held at Nagle's Hotel, and was followed by a dance.

The Southern Star, 10 September 1932.

Lohort Castle, Mallow.

From the John James collection, this postcard of Castle Lohort near Cecilstown was published by Hely's Limited of Dublin. Castle Lohort (also sometimes 'Loghort') was originally a MacCarthy castle, dating from the 1490s (a rebuild of an even older castle), however by the 17th century the MacCarthys had been unburdened of it. In 1641, at the start of the Confederate and Civil Wars, Sir Philip Perceval garrisoned it with a hundred and fifty men, nevertheless rebel Irish forces gained possession of it and held it until May 1650, when Sir Hardress Waller reduced it with a battery of cannon – altogether in the 1640s, it is believed, over 4,500 men died fighting for this stronghold. Afterwards it remained in a state of dilapidation until the middle of the eighteenth century, when Sir Philip Perceval's descendant, the earl of Egmont, restored and refurbished it. The agents of the Egmont estate resided in it during the 19th century, it was the residence of Sir Timothy O'Brien at the beginning of the 20th century and, since the 1920s, that of the McCabe family. This Castle Lohort postcard was never posted.

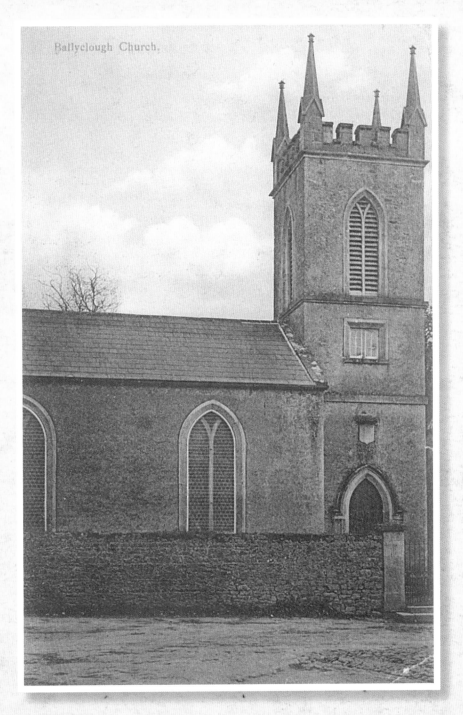

Ballyclough Church.

From the John James collection, this postcard of the Anglican church in Ballyclough was published by Hely's Limited of Dublin. This card was posted in August 1907, to Miss Nellie Mogg at Oakfield, Wembdon, Bridgewater, Somerset, England: "My Dear Nellie," the sender – Biddy – begins, "just a line to let you know I haven't you all forgotten. I hope you are all well. I am having a grand time. This P.C. is a view of one of the churches in our village. I won't forget to write some time again. With best love to you, Biddy."

From the John James collection, this postcard of Banteer was published by Daniel Lawlor, Temperance Hotel, Banteer, Co. Cork. Banteer is a village about 12 kilometres west of Mallow. The postcard was posted in Dublin in August 1929, to Miss Marjory Woodward at Coleburn Distillery, Longman, Morayshire, Scotland: "I hope you are well", the sender – Margaret – begins (writing from Glenavon House, 12 Belvedere Road,

Main Street, Banteer, Co. Cork

Drumcondra, Dublin), "It is a long time now since I have written to you. I am having a lovely holiday. I shall write you a letter soon. Love from Margaret."

THE CASTLE RUINS, MALLOW, CO. CORK.

This Kennelly Photoworks postcard (KenCard Series) of the ruins of Mallow Castle is from the Adrian Healy collection. The card was posted in 1961 to a J. C. Ruane at 1 Edward Street, Brighouse, Yorkshire in England: "91 miles today & I did not intend coming here", the writer, Billy, begins, "When I went to Mass it was very misty and after yesterday I thought it was going to be another hot day. I was going to stay in Macroom and play about all day. It was very hot until about 1:00 pm, then it clouded over a bit; by the time I reached Macroom it was only 2:00 pm. It was

either Cork or Killarney but I headed north to Kanturk. I stopped later and found the nearest place was this 23½ miles away, that was at 3:40. I made it by 5:15. Love Billy" On the banks of the Blackwater River, Mallow Castle is a 16th century fortified house built by Sir Thomas Norreys, Lord President of Munster, before his death in 1599. Afterwards the place passed to his niece, Elizabeth, and her husband, Sir John Jephson, and their descendants. The castle was ruined in the wars of the seventeenth century.

From the John James collection, this Valentine card of St James's, the Anglican parish church in Mallow, was posted in Mallow in May 1910, to a Mrs Sanders at Charleville Park, Charleville, Co. Cork: "My dear Mother", the writer begins (the message is written in pencil and in a poor hand – perhaps because it was written in haste), "Just a line to say that we have just got on the train in Mallow. Hope you are quite well. Much love from Terence."

This Valentine's card from the John James collection was posted in Mallow in August 1906, to a Miss A. Dawson at The Laurels, 20 Claremont Road, Sandymount, Dublin: "Dear A, another picture of Mallow. I passed this place today, Bert." The discovery in 1720s of the curative powers of spa waters in Mallow made the town a significant health and lesuire centre in Ireland in the 18th century. In season, Mallow spa water has a mean temperature of 72° Fahrenheit (about 21° Celsius). In the opinion of eminent medical men of the day, the clear spring water of Mallow was a 'blood purifier' of considerable quality. Modelling itself on Bath in the west of England, the curative season began in April and continued to October. Built over the spa well source, the building pictured dates from 1828, however, designed by George Pain at the request of Mr Charles Jephson (presumably replacing an earlier structure); in its day such a place would have contained a pump room, medical consultation apartments, treatment rooms, reading rooms, etc – all the health spa paraphernalia of 'taking the waters', as they used to say. Today Mallow Spa House is home to the Energy Agency Office, which advises the public on energy conservation and renewable resources.

Castle Kevin, Mallow

From the John James collection, a Valentine's Series card of Castle Kevin, near Mallow, posted in Mallow in February 1911, to a Miss Luck at 6 Grotes Place, Blackheath, London S.E.: "Very many thanks for yours. Will write later. Very busy now. All well here. Am growing a great quantity of S. Peas this year. Please send cuttings for <<illegible>> sometimes. Much love, Yours, W.L.R." It is believed that the 'Kevin' in Castle Kevin derives from the O'Keeffe name, the clan-based power group who once were masters of a stronghold on this site, in particular from 'Caomheen' which means 'the young O'Keeffe.' After the O'Keeffes it was the possession of the (Anglo-Norman) Roche family (later the viscounts of Fermoy) and after that of the (Cromwellian) Thornhills – the building pictured, which dates from the 18th century, is from the Thornhill era.

Clock House, Mallow

From the John James collection, a Valentine's Series card showing the end of Main Street in Mallow with – centre of the picture – Mallow's Clock House (which is actually on the junction of Main Street and Spa Square, on the Spa Square side). The Clock House was designed and built in the 1850s by Sir Denham Orlando Jephson – one of the Jephson family of Mallow Castle – an amateur architect who is said to have designed this structure following his return from a holiday in the Alps. Originally a licensed premises (that is, licensed to sell alcohol – a public house), more recently it has been occupied by Colman Dalton, an accountancy firm. This postcard has never been posted.

Two postcards from the Adrian Healy collection, showing street scenes at Bank Place, Mallow, which is at the upper end of Main Street. The colour card, **above**, is a Lawrence card, and the black and white card, **below**, from half a century later, is a Cardall Company card. These postcards were never posted.

BANK PLACE, MALLOW, CO. CORK

R.C. Church, Mallow

A Valentine's Series postcard of St Mary's, the Roman Catholic church in Mallow, a card from the Adrian Healy collection. On Main Street, Mallow, St Mary's dates from around 1900. This postcard was never posted.

19028   TOWN HALL & FITZGERALDS STATUE, MALLOW

A Signal Series postcard from the John James collection showing Mallow Town Hall and in front of it the FitzGerald monument, which commemorates the work of J.J. Fitzgerald (1872-1906), a local politician instrumental in establishing the Mallow Show, Mallow Urban District Council (of which he was chair until his untimely death at the age of just 33), and Cork County Council. This postcard was never posted.

A card from the Adrian Healy collection which makes a feature of the great flood in Mallow in November 1916. Mallow is notorious for flooding – even today – especially that low-lying area at the bottom of Main Street. The River Blackwater – which runs through the town – in full flood can be a considerable body of water, one which has claimed hundreds of lives down through the ages. This postcard, which does not have a publisher statement, was never posted. (On the flooding in Mallow in November 1916, see J. F. Williamson's 'The great

Mallow Flood, Nov. 17th, 1916.

flood of 17th Nov., 1916, at Mallow' in the *Journal of the Cork Historical and Archaeological Society* for 1917, Vol. XXIII (Ser. 2), pp. 46-9.)

Ten Arch Bridge, Mallow

This Valentine Series postcard is part of a cache of postcards in the Charleville Public Library (on permanent loan from the Charleville Historical Society), which we have been kindly given permission to use. Stamp-hunters have removed the stamp and with it all the information thereby provided, however, this is one of several cards sent to the O'Haras at this address in the early 1900s – see also the Charleville postcards on pp. 171 and

178. This postcard was posted to a Mr R. O'Hara at 21 Churton Street, Belgravia, London SW: "Dear Dad" the writer begins (clearly a child learning the art of written correspondence – the card has been lined for him and the address written out in another's hand) [only part of the message is legible] ". . . much with all my cousins and so is Tim. Mums will write tomorrow had a fine game in martys I got up on the hay cocks."

MALLOW, CO. CORK

From the Adrian Healy collection, a composite of Mallow sights and scenes from the John Hinde company. This postcard has never been posted. On the B-side John Hinde has the following note on Mallow: 'Situated on the north bank of the Blackwater River, Mallow is one of the most prosperous towns in Munster, due to its situation in a rich agricultural region. Mallow was for centuries an important ford on the Blackwater. Up to a century ago it was known as the Bath of Ireland and its spa drew crowds of visitors which gave rise to the popular song The Rakes of Mallow.'

A postcard of the Heatherside Sanatorium, Doneraile, from the Adrian Healy collection, published by J. T. Pratt of Doneraile. Heatherside was an 80-bed treatment centre for patients suffering from tuberculosis ('consumption' as it was commonly termed); Doneraile is a village 9 or 10 kilometres north of Mallow. The card was posted in Buttevant in December 1910, to a Miss T. O' Leary at Lotaville, College Road, Cork: "Dearest T.," the sender – Mille – begins, "Thanks for P.P.C. I am going on A1 How do you like this cold weather. Had a long letter from Alice. She likes London very much. Billie is going to school now too. Good bye, lots of love, from your old chum, Millie."

A postcard of Doneraile Court from the John James collection. There is no publisher statement for this postcard and it was never posted. Doneraile is a village 9 or 10 kilometres north of Mallow. Doneraile was the home and stronghold of the St Ledger family, descendants of Sir William St Ledger, Lord President of Munster in the early 1600s. The St Legers – from 1703 viscounts – retained possession of Doneraile Park and Court down to 1960s. Doneraile Court is an Isaac Rothery building, dating from the mid 18th century; Rothery is also responsible for the Aldworth's Newmarket Court (see p. 149) and Bowen's Court, Elizabeth Bowen's family home (which was demolished in the 1960s).

Duhallow Hounds Meet at Kilmaclenine

Also from the John James collection, a postcard of the Duhallow Hounds meeting at Kilmaclenine, near Buttevant. There is no publisher statement for this card. It was posted in Buttevant on 23 December 1907, to a Mrs Lamb at 33 Penhill Road, Cardiff in Wales: "Wishing Dr & Mrs Lamb & Mr Fuller Ale the compliments of the season." And it is signed "Capt Bolton" who gives (what is presumably) his address as "Woodview, Doneraile, Co. Cork."

Doneraile Church

From the John James collection, a postcard of St Mary's, Doneraile, a church which has been used by the Church of Ireland congregation in the area since it was originally built in the 1630s. A stone slab set in the western side of the tower reads: 'This church was first built by the Rt. Hon. Sir William St. Leger, the Lord President of Munster, *anno Domini* 1633, the Right Honourable Arthur Viscount Doneraile, *anno Domini* 1726.' The spire of St Mary's enjoys fame for the fact that it gave its name to the term 'Steeplechasing.' In 1752 a Mr O'Callaghan and a Mr Edmund Blake raced their mounts 'from the church in Buttevant to the steeple of the St Leger church in Doneraile.' The original spire was blown down in a storm in 1825.

JUSTIN WAS A CITY MAN, a black-coat, down here (where his sister lived) on holiday. Other summer holidays before this he had travelled in France, Germany, Italy: he disliked the chaotic 'scenery' of his own land. He was down here with Queenie this summer only because of the war, which had locked him in. Duty seemed to him better than failed pleasure. His father had been a doctor in this place; now his sister lived on in two rooms in the square – for fear Justin should not be comfortable she had taken a room for him at the hotel. His holiday with his sister, his holiday in this underwater, weedy region of memory, his holiday on which, almost every day, he had to pass the doors of their old home, threatened Justin with a pressure he could not bear. He had to share with Queenie,

as he shared the dolls' house meals cooked on the oil stove behind her sitting room screen, the solitary and almost fairylike world created by her deafness. Her deafness broke down his only defence, talk. He was exposed to the odd, immune, plumbing looks she was forever passing over his face. He could not deflect the tilted blue of her eyes. The things she said out of nowhere, things with no surface context, were never quite off the mark. She was not all solicitude; she loved to tease him.

In her middle-age Queenie was very pretty: her pointed face had the colouring of an imperceptibly faded pink-and-white sweet-pea. This hot summer her artless dresses, with their little lace collars, were mottled over with flowers, mauve and blue. Up the glaring main street she carried a *poult-de-soie* parasol. Her rather dark first-floor rooms faced north, over the square with its grass and lime trees: the crests of great mountains showed above the opposite façades. She would slip in and out on her own errands, calm as a cat, and Justin, waiting for her at one of her windows, would see her cross the square in the noon sunshine with hands laced over her forehead into a sort of porch. This little town, though strung on a through road, was an outpost under the mountains: in its quick-talking, bitter society she enjoyed, to a degree that surprised Justin, her privileged place. She was woman enough to like to take the man Justin around with her and display him; they went out to afternoon or to evening tea, and in those drawing-rooms of tinted lace and intently-staring family photographs, among octagonal tables and painted cushions, Queenie, with her cotton gloves in her lap, well knew how to contribute, while Justin talked, her airy, brilliant, secretive smiling and looking on. For his part, he was man enough to respond to being shown off – besides, he was eased in these breaks in their *tête-a-tête*. Above all, he was glad, for these hours or two of chatter, not to have to face the screen of his own mind, on which the distortion of every one of his images, the war-broken towers of Europe, constantly stood. The immolation of what had been his own intensely had been made, he could only feel, without any choice of his. In the heart of the neutral Irishman indirect suffering pulled like a crooked knife. So he acquiesced to, and devoured, society: among the doctors, the solicitors, the auctioneers, the bank people of this little town he renewed old acquaintanceships and developed new. He was content to bloom, for this settled number of weeks – so unlike was this to his monkish life in the city – in a sort of tenebrous popularity.

He attempted to check his solitary arrogance. His celibacy and his studentish manner could still, although he was past forty, make him acceptable as a young man. In the mornings he read late in his hotel bed; he got up to take his solitary walks; he returned to flick at his black shoes with Queenie's duster and set off with Queenie on their tea-table rounds…

From 'Summer Night' by Elizabeth Bowen, a short story in **Look at all those roses** *(1941).*

MALLOW, CO. CORK

Detail from the Cardall card on p. 157

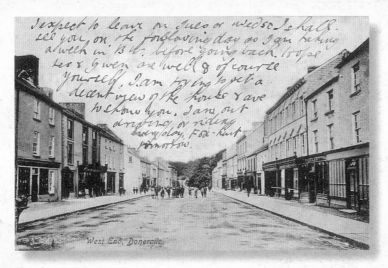

West End, Doneraile.

From the Adrian Healy collection, a postcard showing the main street in Doneraile. There is no publisher statement for this card. It was posted in Buttevant in September 1903, to a Mrs Dowdeswell at 23 Alexandra Road, Bridgewater, Somerset in England; after the place-statement – Saffron Hill, Doneraile, Co. Cork – the sender begins: "You see I happened to go that day and managed to get over alright. The view is part of the village but we are about ½ mile out. I was in Limerick last week, coming back to B.W. early next week. Hope you are all well, P.O." The sender continues on the A-side: "I expect to leave on Tues or Wed so I shall see you on the following day as I am taking a week in BW before going back. I hope Les & Gwen are well & of course yourself. I am trying to get a decent view of the house & ave to show you. I am out driving or riding every day. Fox-hunt tomorrow."

Another Doneraile postcard from the Adrian Healy collection, this one a picture of modernity in rural Cork in the early 1900s. Again the card does not have a publisher statement; it was posted, however, in Ballyvonare (a British military camp in nearby Buttevant) in December 1916, to a Mrs J. Catterill at 7 Somers Place, Regent Street West, Leamington Spa, Warwickshire, England: "Dear Ma & Pa", the writer begins, "Hope you are both well. I am O.K. Can you get me a diary for next year please? Nice today but cold. I do hope that you will have a nice time at Xmas,

West End, Doneraile.

wish I was with you. Best Love, Arch." At the top the young man provides his address in Ireland: "Hut 16, E Company, Command Depot, Ballyvonare, County Cork, Ireland."

The Abbey, Buttevant, Co Cork.

From the John James collection, this Emerald Series postcard was posted in Buttevant in November in 1907, to a Mrs P.J. Ryan at Cooline, Preston Avenue, Newport: "Dear Mrs R", the message begins, "Thanks ever so much for lovely P.C. received some time ago. Excuse me for not acknowledging it sooner. Hope ye are all well over there. We have terrible wet weather here this time past, hope it is not as bad with ye. L. O'Connell." A friary dedicated to St Thomas à Becket, was established at Buttevant in the 1250s. Dissolved, along with all the other monastic establishments in England and Ireland in the 1540s – in the Reformation – the abbey and its lands were subsequently leased to Lord James de Barry, 4th Viscount Buttevant; however, at outbreak of the earl of Desmond's rebellion in the 1570s, Viscount Buttevant joined the rebels and, in the subsequent confiscations of his property, the Buttevant friary, together with its glebe, passed into the hands of the poet Edmund Spencer, an undertaker [of Plantation lands] at Kilcolman Castle, near Doneraile. Throughout the 17th and 18th centuries defiant Franciscan friars continued to attempt to occupy the ruins of the abbey. The river in the foreground is the Awbeg. On the origin of 'Buttevant' – the place-name – see the caption for the Fota card on p. 38.

CATHOLIC CHURCH, BUTTEVANT, CO CORK

From the John James collection, a postcard of St Mary's, the Catholic church in Buttevant, a card published by Macdonald's West End Stores, Buttevant (see p. 168). Designed by Charles Cotterel of Cork, St Mary's was commissioned and built in the 1830s. This postcard was never posted.

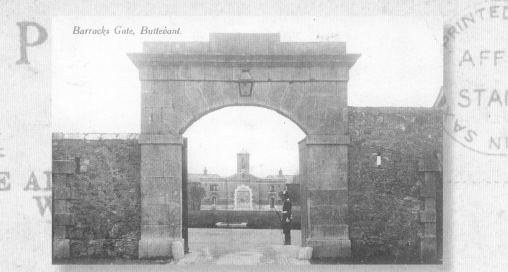

Barracks Gate, Buttevant.

This postcard of the Ballyvonare army barracks, Buttevant, from the John James collection, was published by H. Rosehill of Cork (the correct address for the barracks is Command Depot, Ballyvonare, Buttevant – see the postcard from Archie Catterill to his parents on p. 165). This card was posted in Ballyvonare in 1919 to a Miss R. Sandford at 42 John's Road, Burnley, Lancashire in England: "Dear Rachel", the writer – Howarth – begins, "I am expecting to be home by Monday night, this time final. Yours, Howarth." The British army had a barracks at Buttevant from the early 1800s until the establishment of the Irish Free State in 1922.

MILITARY BARRACKS, BUTTEVANT, CO. CORK.

From the John James collection, another Rosehill postcard of the British army at Buttevant (see card above). This postcard is unstamped but was written out (in very faint pencil) for a Mrs G.J. Davis at 29 Union Road, Tufnell Park, London: "Dear May", the message begins, "I have received your letter and will reply tomorrow. This is a view of the hospital but not the camp. The latter is about 3 miles away in the wilderness. Hope you are quite well. Yours, Geo." In the House of Commons on 14 December 1916 – recorded in *Hansard*, the British parliamentary record – Mr Henry Forster, a spokesman for the War Office, stated that there were nearly four thousand men under medical treatment at Command Depot, Ballyvonare (casualties resulting from the Great War of 1914-18).

Macdonald's West End Stores,° Buttevant Co. Cork.

111948   Macdonald, Publisher, Buttevant. Copyright.

From the John James collection, a
Macdonald's postcard of Macdonald's West
End Stores, Buttevant. In *Guy's Postal
Directory* for 1914, E. Macdonald is listed
under 'Grocers and Vintners' and under
'Hardware Dealers.' The card was posted
in Buttevant in December 1908, to a Mrs
A. Sayer at 19 Airfield Road, Rathgar,
Dublin: "If a pheasant goes to 2b it is for
you. I leave here for Fermoy tonight. Hope
to be back Friday or Saturday. David.
16/12/08."

The Castle, Buttevant. Co.Cork

From the John James collection, a Lawrence postcard of Buttevant Castle, which is also sometimes referred to as Barry Castle or Castle Barry, sometimes also as Bothon Castle, and even King John's Castle – King John of England confirmed William de Barry in his possession of lands on the banks of the Awbeg River that had been granted to William's father, Philip, following the Anglo-Norman invasion of 1185, after which the de Barry family began construction of a castle stronghold on the river's south bank. The building pictured is a rebuild dating from the early 1800s. Today the place is a ruin. This postcard was never posted.

Royal Hotel, Charleville.

A Milton Series postcard from the John James collection featuring the Royal Hotel on Main Street, Charleville, on what looks like Fair Day. This postcard was never posted. 'Charleville' is, of course, 'Charlestown' or 'Charles Town' frenchified: the town was established in the 1660s by Roger Boyle (1621-79), Lord Orrery – third surviving son of Richard Boyle (1566-1643), the earl of Cork – and named in honour of Charles II who, following the implosion of Oliver Cromwell's Commonwealth regime, had been restored to the monarchy in 1660 (Orrery had been a Cromwell supporter, so honouring the restored monarch in this way was part of a rehabilitation campaign).

Three Charleville Fair Day cards from the John James collection, none of which has been posted. The middle and bottom cards are Milton Series postcards, the top one has no publisher statement. Charleville had twelve Fair Days in the calendar year and Market Days on Wednesdays and Saturdays (*Guy's Postal Directory* 1914). On the 17th century origins of the town of Charleville, see the caption for the Royal Hotel card on the preceding page.

Charleville.
Fair Day.

Fair Day, Charleville.

Main Street, Charleville.

Belfort, Charleville, Co. Cork.

This postcard of Belfort House was published by T.J. Riordan of Oriel House, Charleville; it was posted in Charleville in March 1903, to a Mrs R. J. O'Hara at 21 Churton Street, Belgravia, London SW: "Dearest K," the writer begins, "I was delighted to get your letter – to see by it that all are 'A One' and that you enjoyed the concert. Also that you sorted? 'The Dear Little Plant.' I got the parcel last evg, and was surprised at its conts. I am sorry you did not keep the Post Card craze. We are all 1st class. I hope you will like this card. Dot Lincoln is at the Hall door. I am sitting under the tree. Dr Clanchy is in the trap. This man is on the 1st Horse. Paddy Feire, Lord Kenmare's right-hand man is in the background. Paddy & Jack were at school yesterday. Affectionately yours, YHR." Belfort was built in the mid-1700s by Arabella and John Boles Reeves but in the 1800s it became the property of the Clanchy family, builders and developers who built much of the town of Charleville. In the early 1900s it was in the hands of the noted racehorse trainer Dr John Thomas Clanchy. The house and grounds were acquired by the Golden Vale Industrial Estate in the 1950s who demolished the place in the 1970s. This is one of a collection of postcards at Charleville Public Library – a Charleville Historical Society loan deposit – which we have been kindly given permission to use to beef up our representation of this important North Cork town (we are particularly grateful to library's Micheal O'Flaherty who provided a wealth of information relating to the town of Charleville and to the once great houses surrounding the town). This postcard has never been posted.

Memorial, Charleville.

This Milton Series postcard of the IRA monument on Main Street in Charleville is from the John James collection. In May 1921, during the War of Independence, Charleville's Donal O'Brien, an Irish Republican Army volunteer, was executed by the British military authorities; the monument pictured commemorates Donal O'Brien (and others) and the militarized sacrifices made in the cause of the Irish nation-state. The memorial was unveiled in October 1930 by Eamon de Valera, a Nationalist leader of the Easter Rising of 1916 and of the War of Independence, and the then leader of Fianna Fáil, the Republican Party, the political group which were soon to take up the reins of government and go on to become 'the natural party of government' in Ireland (see the *Cork Examiner* extract on the page facing, which reports the gist of Mr de Valera's speech on the occasion). This postcard was never posted.

MR DE VALERA, having pulled the cord that lifted the tricolour from the monument, addressed the gathering:

This stone monument erected to the memory of Donal O'Brien would, he said, remind them all of those men with whom he had taken his stand, and with whom he had joined in making the great sacrifice of giving his young life that Ireland might be free…

…What was their duty, asked Mr De Valera, when they thought of sacrifices like the sacrifice of Donal O'Brien? What had he died for? He died that Ireland might be free – that Ireland might belong to the Irish people, that it might be their very own, without the influences of foreign power. If they were faithful to this man, if they were worthy of his sacrifice, they would, every one of them, say today that the Ireland of the future would be the Ireland for which he died. The men who had raised this monument to Donal O'Brien had done so in loyalty to him and in order that his memory might not be forgotten. They had done even greater service than perpetuate his memory, they had done something for Ireland, because this monument would there stand as a reminder to every one of them that if they were to have an Ireland worth while they should, every one of them, be prepared to make such sacrifices as may be necessary. "This country," he said, "whatever may be the future before it, may be certain of this, that unless we are able to have young men amongst us – unless we are going to have young people who are ready to make such sacrifices as Donal O'Brien made – this country can never realise its ambition to be a great country. No country ever can unless its people are prepared to make sacrifices when called upon. And this stone here in our midst will be something to inspire our young, make them think that there is glory, and great glory, in giving one's life for one's friends and one's country."

As long as this country had families like the O'Briens, he concluded, where the brothers are prepared to stand together and where the mothers and parents would be prepared to give up their sons in order that Ireland might be free, Ireland's future was in safe-keeping. This monument had been given into their keeping, and he knew that the people of the neighbourhood would see to it that it was preserved as it should be, and that everyone that passed it by would not only say a prayer for Donal O'Brien, and for those who had given up their lives, but for the achievement of that object for which they had died, and that those purposes would be finally secured. (Applause.)

The Lee Pipers' Band played the National Anthem, after which "The Last Post" was sounded, while all present stood in silence, the men's heads bared.

Cork Examiner, *6 October 1930. (Éamon de Valera grew up in nearby Bruree – just over the border in County Limerick – and, in his teens, attended the Christian Brothers School in Charleville.)*

Convent of Mercy, Charleville.

A Milton Series postcard of the Convent of the Congregation of the Sisters of Mercy in Charleville, a card from a collection of postcards in the Charleville Public Library – a Charleville Historical Society loan deposit – which we have been kindly given permission to use. This postcard has never been posted. The convent building pictured dates from the late 1830s – the Convent of Mercy in Charleville was founded by the Venerable Catherine McAuley (1777-1841), founder of the Congregation of the Sisters of Mercy.

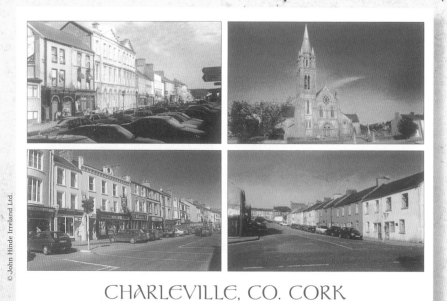

© John Hinde Ireland Ltd.

CHARLEVILLE, CO. CORK

From the Adrian Healy collection, a John Hinde composite of Charleville scenes (photography by Jim Noonan). On the B-side the John Hinde company have the following brief note on Charleville: 'CHARLEVILLE, CO. CORK, situated on the main road between Cork and Limerick in the heart of the renowned agricultural region of the Golden Vale.' This postcard has never been posted.

R.C. Church and Parochial House, Charleville.

Milton Series postcards of Holy Cross Church, the Roman Catholic temple in Charleville, cards from a collection of postcards in the Charleville Public Library – a Charleville Historical Society loan deposit – which we have been kindly given permission to use. These postcards have never been posted. The foundation stone of this Gothic-Revival church was laid by Dr Robert Browne, bishop of Cloyne, in September 1898. The foundation stone names M.A. Hennessy as architect and D. Creedon as builder. The stained-glass windows are from the workshop of the celebrated Harry Clarke. The church was consecrated and officially opened in May 1902 by Dr Browne (the belfry and spire not completed until 1910).

R.C. Church, Charleville.

This postcard of Binchy Park (also known as Knight's Lodge) is a Milton Series postcard from a collection of postcards in the Charleville Public Library – see caption for the Belfort House card on p. 171. The postcard was never posted. Originally built by Robert Featherstone in the 1790s, the house became known as Knight's Lodge because, in the first half of the 19th

Binchey's Park, Charleville.

century, it was occupied by Thomas Knight Roche, a lawyer in nearby Charleville. In the 1920s the estate was purchased by Owen Binchy – the son in the legal partnership of James Binchy & Son of Main Street, Charleville, a family firm of general law practitioners still on the high street in Charleville, now in its fourth generation. The property, apparently, continues to be in the hands of the Binchy family.

Sanders Park, Charleville, Co. Cork.

This postcard of Sanders Park is a Milton Series postcard from a collection of postcards in the Charleville Public Library which we have been kindly given permission to use – see caption for the Belfort House card on p. 171. The postcard was never posted. Originally known as Deer Park, and belonging to the Boyles of Charleville Manor (Boyles as in the earls of Cork), the thousand or so acres that constituted what became the Sanders Park estate was acquired by William Sanders (on a perpetual lease) in 1697. The house pictured, however, dates from the late 18th century. The last of the Sanders family to live at Sanders Park was Robert Massey Dawson Sanders, Justice of the Peace and High Sherriff for the County of Cork. After his death Sanders Park became the property of the Binchy family in the early 1900s, the family of the writer Maeve Binchy, whose father was born here. The property suffered a decline in fortunes in the latter part of the 20th century – at one point the house was divided into bedsit apartments – it is now an abandoned ruin.

Protestant Church, Charleville.

This postcard of the Anglican church in Charleville is from a collection of postcards in Charleville Public Library which we have been kindly given permission to use – see caption for the Belfort House card on p. 171. Charleville Library, by the by, is now housed in this building, which in the 1960s and 70s slipped into disuse as a church and was abandoned altogether before being resurrected in the late 1980s as the county library outlet in the town). T. J. Riordan of [Oriel House] Charleville is identified as the publisher but the card is clearly a Valentine production (the B-side is crowned with the Valentine trademark):

Valentine's used to do this, apparently, as a sales and marketing tactic – identify the local vendor as the publisher when printing the cards, but in reality these were wholly Valentine productions, which Mr and Mrs T. J. O'Riordan were merely retailing. The O'Riordan's were merchants in the town – in *Guys' Postal Directory* (1914) they are listed as grocers, confectioners, builders, and stationers. Mrs T. J. O'Riordan is also listed under 'Fancy Warehouse, etc', which, presumably, is a gift shop – china, glassware, clocks and trinkets – with maybe fabrics (cushions and ribbons) and toys as well.

Fortlands, Charleville

From the John James collection, this postcard of Fortlands House, a farmhouse just outside of Charleville, is a Milton Series card. The postcard was never posted.

The Stables, Lisnagree, Charleville, Co. Cork

Lisnagree was an estate belonging to Valentine Charles Browne, 5th earl of Kenmare, which was given over to the Marshall family, the earl's land agent. This postcard is one of a collection of postcards in Charleville Public Library which we have been kindly given permission to use – see caption for the Belfort House card on p. 171. It was posted in Charleville in November 1903, to a Mrs R. J. O'Hara at 21 Churton Street, Belgravia, London: "Dearest K, Butter sent parcelled – post this Evg. It is grand & fresh and we hope you will like it. This was a very big Fair Day. I was working hard, but am feeling grand, Thank God. Will write tomorrow and give all latest news. Best love to the dear Old frds, | Affectionately yours, TeeJay."

EASTLANDS

A Girl Can't Remain
Single Long
AT MITCHELSTOWN.

A Millar & Lang "National Series" postcard from the John James collection (see also the card on p. 184). This postcard was never posted; however, on the B-side, in pencil, the following is written (in the same hand as the writing on the B-side of the card on p.184): "For Alfie also / cards."

© John Hinde Irreland Ltd.

Mitchelstown, Co Cork

From the Adrian Healy collection, a John Hinde composite of modern-day street scenes in Mitchelstown (photography by Jack Hyland). This postcard was never posted. On the B-side the John Hinde company has the following note on the town and its surrounds: 'Mitchelstown, Co. Cork, is situated at the south-west corner of the Galtee Mountains, near the Tipperary border, and is the centre of a busy agricultural district. Mictchelstown has a unique 18th century townscape, has long enjoyed the reputation of being 'The Home of Good Food', and is associated nationally and internationally with quality dairy and other agricultural productions.'

Mitchelstown.

Galtee Mountains from Market Square.

A Fergus O'Connor card of part of the market square in Mitchelstown (with the Galtee mountains in the background) from the Adrian Healy collection. This postcard was never posted.

The Rectory, Mitchelstown.   (Conche)

A postcard from the John James collection showing the Church of Ireland Rectory in Mitchelstown, published by D.J. Lyons of Mitchelstown. This postcard was posted in Lismore in County Waterford in 1910, to a Miss A. O'Brien at the Income Tax Office on Main Street, Lismore (however, 'Income Tax Office', 'Main Street', and 'Lismore' have been crossed out and replaced with 'C/o Mrs Scanlon, Main St, Dungarvan, Co. Waterford') "Dear Agnes", the message begins, "Received your PC this morning. Willie is quite well. He could not receive you owing to pressure of business. His boss is away – Tom."

King Street, Mitchelstown

A Valentine card from the John James collection showing King Street in Mitchelstown, with – in the distance – the spire of the Roman Catholic church. This postcard was never posted.

POST CARD

THIS SPACE MAY BE USED
FOR COMMUNICATION
IN THE BRITISH ISLES ONLY.
(Post Office Regulation.)

THE ADDRESS ONLY TO BE
WRITTEN HERE.

Miss Compton
36 Bel

Mitchelstown Castle from Warren Hill.

A postcard from the John James collection showing Mitchelstown Castle (sometimes also known as 'Kingston Castle'), seat of the earls of Kingston. Between 1776 and 1825, Mitchelstown Castle and its grounds were laid out (to a landscape design probably by John Webb – Webb had worked as an assistant to the celebrated English landscaper, Lancelot 'Capability' Brown). The Mitchelstown Castle demesne was 502 hectares (1,240 acres). It incorporated fishponds, extensive farm buildings, walled gardens, stables, an ice house, bridges, woodlands, avenues, and so on and on, all enclosed by a 10.5 kilometre (6.5 miles) three-metre high, limestone wall. The Kingston castle at Mitchelstown was burned down by the IRA in 1922 (during the Civil War which followed the nationalist War of Independence); the cut stone was afterwards sold to the Cistercian monks at Mount Melleray Abbey in County Waterford, and used to build a new monastery. Mitchelstown Co-operative Agricultural Society built a milk-processing factory on the castle site, which it had purchased together with some of the demesne lands surrounding it. The site is now owned by Dairygold Co-op. This postcard was posted in January 1906, to a Miss Compton at 36 Belgrave Mews South, Belgrave Square, in London. The message is in the Irish language (these are all phrase-book type expressions): 'Bail ó Dhia ort má sé do thoil é' (May God be with you please). 'Go mbeannuighidh Dia dhuit', which means something similar. 'Beannacht leat' means goodbye (although, strictly speaking, it translates as 'peace be with you'). And 'Seaghán Ua Riain' is the writer's name.

THE KINGSTONS built modern Mitchelstown, originally a holding of the Condons…by 1614 all these old lordships had come down to one Margaret FitzGibbon, whose daughter married Sir John King, later Lord Kingston of Mitchelstown.

In 1786 a later Margaret King received her lessons in Mitchelstown Castle from Mary Wollstonecraft (1759-97) who had written but not yet published *Thoughts on the Education of Daughters* (1787). The revolutionary feminist was to marry the radical William Godwin but neither revolution nor radicalism could save her from the old-fashioned septicaemia which killed her after the birth of her daughter Mary (1797-1851). The younger Mary married Percy Bysshe Shelley and wrote *Frankenstein, or the Modern Prometheus* (1818).

Although Mary Wollstonecraft stayed with the Kings for only two years her impact was considerable. The fourteen year old Margaret was enthralled by her and was later to develop, to the dismay of her husband, from whom she eventually separated, an eccentric political philosophy of her own which allowed her to support Republican and other causes in Ireland and abroad. In Italy Margaret became a friend of Shelley and his wife Mary…

[The old Mitchelstown castle] was considered too small for the third earl, known locally as 'Big George.' It was demolished and replaced by an enormous building designed by the Pain brothers, beggaring the family. George's son, Edward, Viscount Kingsborough (1795-1837) was an antiquarian who published *The Antiquities of Mexico* (1830) at a personal cost of £32,000; he died from typhus while imprisoned as a bankrupt in Dublin's Marshalsea only two years before he would have inherited the family estate.

The great castle of Mitchelstown was burned down by the IRA in 1922, its stone taken for the building of the abbey of Mount Melleray at Cappoquin, Co. Waterford, its very site now marked by a large creamery:

"In virtue of this being a garden party, and of the fact that it was not actually raining, pressure was put on guests to proceed outside… Wind raced around the castle terraces, naked under the Galtees; grit blew into the ices; the band clung with some trouble to its exposed place.

"It was an afternoon when the simplest person begins to anticipate memory – this Mitchelstown garden party, it was agreed, would remain in everyone's memory as historic. It was, also, a more final scene than we knew, ten years hence it was all to seem like a dream – and the castle itself would be a few bleached stumps on the plateau. Today, the terraces are obliterated and grass grows where salons were… The unseen descent of the sun behind the clouds sharpens the bleak light; the band, having throbbed out 'God Save the King', packs up its wind-torn music and goes home."

Thus, in *Bowen's Court*, Elizabeth Bowen remembers the first day of the First World War, when, as a fifteen year old, her only anxiety was whether or not the Mitchelstown garden party would be cancelled.

Extract from 'Mitchelstown' in **The Lie of the Land: Journeys through Literary Cork,** *by Mary Leland (Cork University Press, 1999).*

BEST WISHES.
FROM MITCHELSTOWN.

MAY FORTUNE RICHLY
DOWER
YOUR LIFE WITH
MUCH SUCCESS,
AND ON YOU SEND
A SHOWER
OF ALL THINGS
THAT CAN BLESS.

A Millar & Lang "National Series" postcard from the John James collection. This postcard was never posted, however, on the B-side, in pencil, the following is written: "For Alfie, with best wishes, from his loving brother, Harry." See also card on p. 179.

A Valentine card from the John James collection showing the dwellings on Mullbery Lane in Mitchelstown. This postcard was never posted.

A postcard from the John James collection of 'The College, Mitchelstown' (sometimes also identified as 'Kingston College'), published by T.L. Morrissey of Mitchelstown. This is not a 'college' in the sense of an educational institution, rather it is a cluster of dwellings as in something like a housing association – 'college' can be used to describe any group of people living together in community. The College was constructed and endowed in the 1760s by James, 4th Baron Kingston. It consists of thirty small terraced (non-identical) houses grouped around a square, and includes a chapel and a community room. Originally the foundation was intended for former tenants of Lord Kingston's estate – the Mitchelstown Castle estate (see pp. 182-3) – nearby. The College dwellings are now occupied by retired people from all walks of life and from all parts of Ireland (and beyond). This postcard was posted in Croydon, south London, in March 1910, sent to a Miss E. Green at Hillthorpe, Sydenham: "Dear Edie", the writer writes, "Thank you for your letter. There's a train 8.23 and another 9.47 from the Palace. Love, Mother." (The 'Palace', of course, being Crystal Palace, south of London.)

A postcard from the Adrian Healy collection showing a scene on Main Street in Kilworth. Kilworth is a village about two kilometres north of Fermoy. This postcard, published by W. O'Connell, Sationer, Fermoy, was never posted.

From the John James collection, a Valentine postcard of Castlehyde House near Fermoy. Castlehyde House on the banks of the river Blackwater was originally built to the design of Davis Ducart in the 1750s, commissioned by the Hyde family (from whom Douglas Hyde, the first president of an independent Ireland, was descended); despite alterations and renovations by succeeding proprietors it is still regarded as one of the finest examples of the Irish Georgian country house style. Castlehyde House is presently the possession of Michael Flatley, of 'Riverdance' and 'Lord of the Dance' fame. This postcard was never posted.

The Bridge, Fermoy

From the John James collection, a Valentine postcard of the bridge crossing the Blackwater at Fermoy (which dates from the 1860s). The postcard was posted in Fermoy in 1912, to a Miss J. Evans, at Killua Castle, Clonmellon, Co. Meath: "Thanks for your letter, received safe", the writer begins under the place-statement "Royal Hotel | Fermoy." "We came here Sat evg and are going back tomorrow, Monday. Lovely weather. The wedding takes place tomorrow morning, great style for it. I think we are going to Rosslare soon, perhaps in a week's time. With Love from your loving sister." And then there is a PS written in a corner: "Will write you a letter soon but I expect I will be very busy next week. E."

WEST QUAY, FERMÓY.

From the John James collection, a Woolstone Brothers' (Milton "Glazette" Series) card showing a wintery West Quay in Fermoy. This postcard was never posted.

PATRICK STREET. FERMOY. CO. CORK

From the John James collection, a Cardall company card featuring Patrick Street in Fermoy. The card was posted in Fermoy in 1963, to a Mr & Mrs Lea, Tritonville Road, Sandymount, Dublin: "Having a nice holiday. Weather is lovely and warm. We have been to see quite a few places. Hope you are both well. M. Symes."

FERMOY.1417.W.L

Another postcard of Fermoy Bridge from the John James collection, this one from the Lawrence company (see also p. 187). This postcard was never posted.

FERMOY was the scene in 1930 of an Irish battle quite different from any of those which are recorded through the centuries as having shaken the country – one in which Starlings were the invaders, and Rooks the defenders. The episode is one which reflects creditably on the capacity in the domain of military tactics of the Rook, which one is rather inclined to look on as a stupid noisy bird. The field of battle was the tops of two groups of tall trees, one in Fermoy and one on an island in the Blackwater below Fermoy bridge. Both of these places were used for nesting in spring, and for roosting in winter, by the Rooks, which congregated nightly to the number of several hundreds, accompanied by friendly Jackdaws. A mile and a half away, in a wood of young conifers, Starlings had a great roost, and each winter evening flocks estimated at 10,000 or 12,000 passed thither over the town of Fermoy. On the evening of 2nd November, however, after the Rooks had retired for the night, the homing Starlings hesitated, wheeled round and round the town for a while, and then suddenly poured down into the Rooks' dormitories. The Rooks protested vigorously and noisily, rising and flying around wildly, but the Starlings merely returned the owners' bad language and refused to budge. After some hours of recrimination things became quiet.

Each night for a week exactly the same thing happened, but on 9th November there was a surprise. Until the arrival of the Starlings everything was quiet, but when the intruders appeared, up rose not the usual Rook population of some 300, but a black mass estimated at 1,500 to 2,000 birds, with tremendous cawing. They did not attack the Starlings, but hovered, densely packed, a few feet above the tree-tops. Four times the horde of Starlings poured down, four times the Rooks rose and renewed their dense barrage. The Starlings in the end admitted defeat and made off to their own pine-wood.

One section of the Starlings held on until 11th November, when they also were finally defeated by the same tactics. The Rooks were taking no chances and remained in abnormal numbers until 14th November, when they gradually reduced their garrison until the population was again normal. The Starlings made no further attempt, and eventually left the neighbourhood altogether.

The most remarkable thing about the incident was… the deliberate summoning and arrival of reinforcements on the part of the Rooks, and the clever form of passive resistance by which they vanquished their smaller but vigorous and aggressive cousins. In a general rough-and-tumble, numbers of starlings could have slipped through, but the dense stratum of Rooks prevented this effectually, and the Starlings were completely outmaneuvered without a blow being struck. But how did Rooks arrange for large reinforcements, and how did they think out and maintain their clever ruse?

*From Robert Lloyd Praeger's **The way that I went: an Irishman in Ireland** (Hodges, Figgis & Co., Dublin; Methuen & Co., London, 1939).*

Three postcards of the British army barracks at Fermoy. The barracks was on 16.5 acres of grounds and at full compliment provided accommodation for about 200 officers and nearly 3,000 men. Originally established in the early 1800s, during the Wars with Revolutionary France, the town of Fermoy expanded around these facilities, retaining its British military connections up until 1922, when the Irish Free State was established. The Fermoy barracks, by the by, were burned out after the British troops left, the empty complex was burned by IRA Irregulars (IRA people refused to accept the Anglo-Irish Treaty of 1921 which established only a 26-county Irish Free State, which is to say an Ireland without six of the counties of Ulster), to prevent the Free State troops occupying it; that is, it was burned out as part of the Civil War.

Old Barracks, Fermoy

All three postcards are from the John James collection, none of them were posted. The Old Barracks card (top) has no publisher statement. The New Barracks card (center) appears to be published by 'E. Lindsey, Stationer, Fermoy.' And the burned out barracks card is embossed with 'R. Stritch, Fermoy', which may be the publisher.

THE NEW BARRACKS, FERMOY

NEW BARRACS FERMOY AFTER FIRE.

Chums of the R.W.F. Moore Park.

From the John James collection, this Royal Welch Fusiliers card was never posted. On the B-side it is stamped 'L. Edwards, Fermoy', who may be the publisher or perhaps the retailer.

Moore Park was a Cadet training camp associated with the Fermoy army barracks. This card, which has no publisher-statement and was never posted, is from the John James collection.

THE CAMP.   MOORE PARK.

Also from the John James collection, this postcard has no publisher statement and was never posted. On the B-side of this card is written, in pencil, 'E. Coy. 1st Bn The King's Regt | Winners of the Silver "Shooting Cup" 1912 | Photographer Couche (?) Fermoy." *Guy's Postal Directory* for 1914 lists a Jeffrey Couche as having a photographic studio on Francis Street, Fermoy.

WITH FONDEST LOVE.
FROM FERMOY.

'Tis only a
simple card
I send,
To remind you
of an absent
friend,

To awaken hosts
of memories
dear,
And wish you
Joy from far
and near.

A Millar & Lang "National Series" postcard from the John James collection. This postcard was never posted; however, on the reverse is written "To my Darling May, from Chris."

A Signal Series postcard of the Bishop Murphy School in Fermoy from the John James collection. This postcard was never posted. The Signal Series of postcards were published by E. & S. Ltd of Dublin and Belfast (pre-1917). Bishop Timothy Murphy was the Roman Catholic bishop of Cloyne from 1850 to 1856; a Christian Brothers School, the Bishop Murphy Memorial School was originally established in the 1860s by Bishop Murphy's successor Dr William Keane, bishop of Cloyne, 1856-74.

Another Signal Series postcard, from the John James collection (see caption above). Again this postcard was never posted. The Loretto Convent School in Fermoy dates from the 1850s when Bishop Timothy Murphy of Cloyne invited the Loretto sisters at Rathfarnham in Dublin to open a school for the education of young girls in the town.

A Valentine postcard from the John James collection featuring the Church of Ireland in Fermoy, which is Christ Church on Church Hill. This postcard has never been posted.

From the John James collection a W. O'Connell postcard featuring a couple boating on the Blackwater river near the Carrickabrack railway viaduct. On the B-side 'W. O'Connell, Stationer, Fermoy' is printed where the publisher statement is usually to be found. *Guy's Postal Directories* for 1907 and 1914 do not list a W. O'Connell among the printers and stationers in the town, however, they do list a McConnell & Cruise printing firm on Patrick Street, and the residential portion of the directories list a W. O'Connell on the same street – street numbers are not provided. This postcard has never been posted.

Upper Main Street, Castletownroche, Co. Cork

Lawrence, Publisher, Dublin

POST CA

NEWTONVILLE
NOV 25
8 PM
1959
MASS.

Mrs. Harold J. Manning
5 Pine Ridge Road
Wellesley Hills, Mass.

Seat #3

Dough Re Me

Box 5000

New York 46,

N. Y.

The A-side and B-side of a Lawrence card from the John James collection featuring part of the main street in Castletownroche, which is a village about 12 kilometres west of Fermoy (about halfway between Mallow and Fermoy). The 'Castletownroche' name is from the late 13th century when the Anglo-Norman family of de la Roche established a fortress here.

TOO BUSY TO WRITE.
AT YOUGHAL.

A Bradford Post Card Company postcard from the John James collection. The card was posted in Youghal in 1908, to a Miss H. Gallagher, William Street, Galway: "Here with 5,000 children!" is all the message says; it is signed "HG."

MOST of my readers have heard of Youghal – that quaint little seaport of southern Ireland – in whose crowded ways and narrow alleys linger so many traces of another age; of days when the Desmonds swept through its streets in feudal state, or of the later time when Raleigh mused under his myrtle trees beneath the shadow of its wondrous old church. Though not lovely, like other Irish watering-places, yet it possesses a certain individuality which saves it from being vulgarized by the welcome, if motley, horde of pleasure-seekers who descend upon the town ere the first pinks have opened in the garden borders, and loiter on until the last red geraniums have ceased blazing on the window sills. One feels it has a stern past behind its new stucco, and was not called into existence by a flourish of bathers' towels or a caprice of fashion.

In summer all things are beautiful... The slumberous waters of the great bay flash and sparkle in the sunlight, reflecting the luminous blue of a cloudless Irish sky. Tawny sand and lichen-stained rock blend their varying tints upon the low-lying shores that gradually recede in melting perspective to the low green hills rolling away northward, and the line of "villas", extending from Clay Castle to the railway station, gleam radiant in fresh paint... On such days the place looks at its best, and is best viewed from the bay, where one may pass a pleasant hour on the gentle swell of the ocean, with few sounds to break the stillness save the babble of the people on the sands or the patter of English musketry from the rifle ranges opposite.

From 'Cambia Carty' in **Cambia Carty and other stories** *(1907), by William Buckley.*

Clock Gate, Main Street, Youghal, Co. Cork, Ireland.   Colour Photo by John Hinde, F.R.P.S.

A John Hinde card from the Adrian Healy collection. This postcard was never posted. On the B-side the John Hinde company has the following note on Youghal: 'Youghal is one of the foremost seaside resorts of Co. Cork, and is finely situated at the mouth of the Blackwater river, with a fine strand and every holiday amenity. Youghal was occupied by the Danes, and then by the Normans, receiving its first charter from King John, who was supplied by the town with three fighting ships. Youghal was fortified with walls and towers, most of which still remain. Of these the renovated Clock Gate, which spans the main street, is the most picturesque.'

The Strand, Youghal, Co. Cork, Ireland.   Colour Photo by John Hinde, F.R.P.S.

Another John Hinde card from the Adrian Healy collection. This card was posted in Youghal in 1967, to a Mr & Mrs Johnston & Family at 37 Upper Coachill Road, Belfast 15, in Northern Ireland: "We're not exactly having a heat-wave", the writer begins, "but are really enjoying caravan life. Our caravan is only a few yards from the shore & right beside the path to it, so the children are loving it. We've been to Youghal a number of times, and last week we went to Cork. Next to us we had a family from Gilnahirk & 3 others on the Sili too. Hope you are all well. Lovely to get your letter. See you all soon. Love, Jim & Maureen etc."

The Old Town, Youghal

CINEMA SHIPS, YOUGHAL, CO. CORK

Two postcards from the Adrian Healy collection; the Cinema Ships postcard is a Cardall Company card, posted in July 1960 to Mr J. Ruane at 1 Edward Street, Brighouse, Yorkshire: "Thursday, 4.15", the message begins, "Taken all day to get here. It has been hot and sunny with the wind at my back. Looking for a bed now. Love, Billy." Many of the exterior New Bedford scenes in John Huston's 1956 film version of Herman Melville's classic novel *Moby Dick* (1851) were filmed in Youghal. John Huston directed the film and wrote the screenplay – along with Ray Bradbury – and Gregory Peck and Orson Welles were two of the production's 'name' actors. The town's harbour area, in front of Linehan's bar (since renamed The Moby

Dick), was used as New Bedford's harbour. Several locals appear as extras in the ship's departure scene. Youghal's lighthouse also appears in the scene of the 'Pequod' putting to sea on her ill-fated voyage. The other card (**top**) is a Valentine Series production; it was posted in Sixmilebridge in County Clare in September 1904, to Mrs Ward at Overton House, Brown Street, Salisbury, England: "Sixmilebridge, Saturday" the writer begins (in what is a very poor hand) "Arrived home safely <<*illegible*>> to Mayfield. Had nice journey. Thanks for pretty P.C. so glad to get. All on my return <<*illegible*>> Much love, xxx's from H.S."

AT YOUGHAL.

If I stay another week
I'll bust this bally machine !

From the John James collection, a "Comique" Series postcard from the Inter-Art Company, Florence House, Barnes, London. The postcard was never posted.

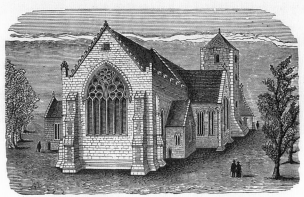

St. Mary's Collegiate Church, Youghal (11th Century).
Printed from Old Woodcut.   (Copyright) by W. G. Field.

This postcard of St Mary's church in Youghal is from the Adrian Healy collection. The postcard does not have a publisher statement and has never been posted. The site of St Mary's in Youghal is an ancient site of Christian worship – going back to a monastic settlement established by St Declan of Ardmore (c. 450). The roof timbers of St Mary's have been carbon dated to the 1170s. There was an early 13th century re-building of the church under the direction of the Masters of four local guilds of masons, whose marks are to be found on the pillars of the gothic arches.

In 1464, with the foundation of 'Our Lady's College of Yoghill' by Thomas FitzGerald, 7th earl of Desmond (proprietor of Youghal and Lord Deputy of Ireland), St Mary's was made a Collegiate Church for the purpose of training seminarians. Following the English Reformation, however, the church and its assets came into the control of the Established Anglican church. The Roman Catholic population was obliged to quit the premises and conduct their services elsewhere, in private or – a little later – cease and desist altogether.

There is no publisher statement on this postcard from the John James collection, it just says 'Made in Austria.' The card was posted in Youghal in November 1908, to a Miss M. Keyes at 4 Caerau Road, Newport, Wales: "Dearest Maggie, thanks for pretty PC. Please forgive me for not answering before now! Am in Youghal today. Saw no one interesting. Hope to hear from you soon again. Best love to all, not forgetting Agnus. Your fond cousin, M."

From the Adrian Healy collection, a Hely's postcard showing the interior of St Mary's, the Anglican church in Youghal. This postcard was never posted.

IN St MARY'S church on this damp afternoon a film crew are setting up their gear. In the vestry there are photographs of previous rectors, among them Canon Darling, good at tennis in 1934, who accidently lighted a box of matches when meaning only to light a cigarette, whose cat sipped whiskey from his glass and staggered drunkenly about. The camera crew wear bright anoraks, but speak in low voices, as is fitting in these surroundings. A coffin rests on a trolley in front of the altar steps, a candle in a massive candlestick at each corner. The varnish of the coffin gleams, highlighting the yellow wood. Such hefty candles in this Protestant church do not look right…

"An uphill struggle," the clergyman complains, referring to the problems of old buildings and keeping everything up. He's dressed to take a service, and I wonder who has died. In fact, no-one has; the yellow coffin's empty. "Some kind of documentary", the obliging cleric explains, his tone of voice suggesting there has been a fee. "I wonder if I should tell them those candles shouldn't be there?"

From William Trevor's **Excursions in the Real World** *(Hutchinson, 1993).*

From the John James collection, an Emerald Series postcard from the Irish Pictorial Postcard Company featuring the memorial in St Mary's church in Youghal to Richard Boyle (1566-1643), the first earl of Cork – not infrequently referred to as "the Great Earl of Cork." Boyle was certainly a formidable character: according to his own account – a second son – he left a relatively modest home in Canterbury with £27 to his name, a degree from Cambridge University, a ring worth £10, his 'rapier and dagger', and a couple of letters of introduction and, in Ireland – at a time when the old Gaelic order was being systematically dismantled and replaced with a "New English", Reformation establishment – Boyle made a fortune, a vast robber-baron fortune. Before the end of his long life Boyle had become one of the great lords of Early Modern Europe, so much so – for example – that his relentless enmity undermined and eventually brought down Thomas Wentworth, the earl of Strafford, King Charles I's vice-regent in Ireland (in part Wentworth's policies in Ireland sought to curb Boyle's grasping activities). In 1641, Wentworth was beheaded, for treason, which in turn, not long after, led directly to the fall of the king himself (also beheaded). In the shark-infested waters of 16th and 17th century power-plays, the earl of Cork was one shark you didn't want to tangle with, no matter who you were. This card was posted in Epsom in Surrey in 1904, to a Miss W. Hooker at Station House in Wool, near Wareham in Dorset: "Dear W, a line to ask what you would most care for on our visit. Let me know early. Best love to all. Has Dad heard anything? I trust all are well, Jack."

Emerald Series   EARL OF CORK'S TOMB.

Myrtle Grove, at one time the residence of the Warden of Our Lady's College of Youghal (see the St Mary's postcards on pp. 200 and 201). Following the English Reformation, however, the church and college and the associated assets came into the control of the Established (Anglican) church, and the rights and tithes and offices and appurtenances of the college were traded among the 'New English' elite – Elizabethan buccaneer Sir Walter Raleigh, for example, lived in Myrtle Grove while he was Mayor of Youghal in the 1580s. Myrtle Grove is regarded as the finest example of a Tudor house in Ireland. This postcard, which is from the John James collection, does not have a publisher statement and was never posted.

From the Adrian Healy collection, this Lawrence postcard was posted in Youghal in August 1926, to a Miss Downing at Cumberland Terrace, Birr, County Offaly: "Our house is all red & is facing the sea," the message begins "we get a great blow. I bathe nearly every day. How are you keeping? Trust very well & not too hard worked. Love to all, Rory & Alice."

Presentation Convent Youghal Co.Cork

A Lawrence postcard, featuring the Presentation Convent in Youghal from the Adrian Healy collection. It was posted in Youghal in August 1907, to a Miss H. Punch, Ballyhindon House, Fermoy: "I arrived safely yesterday", the message begins. "It has been raining all day, but is getting nice now. Love to all, MP." The Presentation Sisters had a convent at Youghal from the 1840s up until the 1990s, a school which was renowned for its Irish lace productions – known as Youghal Lace or Point d'Irlande.

YEW TREES, MYRTLE GROVE, YOUGHAL.

A "Philco" Publishing Company postcard from the John James collection featuring a man in a great coat among the Yew trees at Myrtle Grove (on Myrtle Grove, see the Myrtle Grove postcard on p. 203). This postcard was never posted.

A Guy & Co. postcard from the John James collection featuring Powers Terrace in Ballycotton, which is a seaside village along the coast from Youghal (south of Midleton, the village is equidistant from Youghal to the east and Cork city to the west, about 25 kilometres from either). Stamp-hunters have removed the stamp and with it all of the information that can be had thereby, however, the card was posted to a Rev. J. O'Keefe C.C., Kanturk: "Arrived last evening", the writer begins the message under the time-and-place statement 'Sea View Hotel, Tuesday'; "Nice run from Aghadoe. Fr Curtin was asking for you. Raining to-day. Pretty large number here only a few Cloyne men. Best Wishes, E.G."

From the Adrian Healy collection, a Mac Publications postcard showing the fishing pier at Ballycotton. This postcard was never posted.

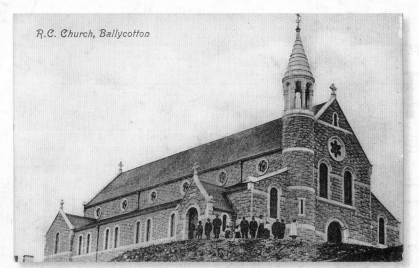

R.C. Church, Ballycotton

From the John James collection, a postcard of the Roman Catholic church in Ballycotton. This card, published by G. Ludlow of Ballycotton, was never posted.

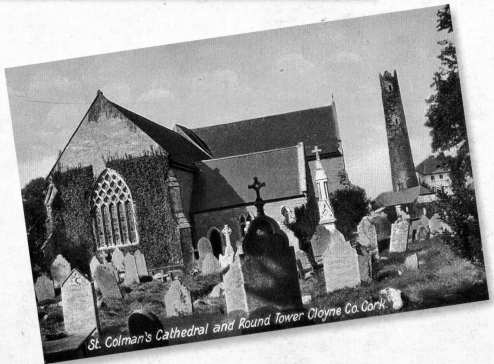

St. Colman's Cathedral and Round Tower Cloyne Co. Cork.

A Lawrence postcard from the Adrian Healy collection. This postcard was never posted. St Coleman's Cathedral in Cloyne is a cathedral of the Church of Ireland (since the Reformation). St Colman founded a monastic settlement at Cloyne in the 560s. Cloyne was recognised as a diocese at the Synod of Kells in 1152. The present church dates from 1250, built on the site of older church buildings. (A Roman Catholic cathedral of St Colman was built at Queenstown/Cobh at the end of the nineteenth century.)

BETWEEN Rostellan on the water's edge and Ballymaloe's long pastures and hillside woods is the cathedral town of Cloyne, where one of Ireland's finest remaining round towers is found. The town has the reputation as the last ministry and home of philosopher and bishop George Berkeley (1685-1753). Born near Thomastown, Co. Kilkenny, Berkeley was a student and then a fellow of Trinity College, Dublin, where he established himself as an intellectual observer and commentator with publications such as *A New Theory of Vision* (1707) and *A Treatise Concerning the Principles of Human Knowledge* (1713).

His Utopian scheme for establishing in Bermuda an ideal community where native young men would be trained as candidates for the Anglican priesthood won attention and support when he began to promote it in the 1720s. By then his reputation as a scholar was made; a friend of Swift, of Pope and Addison, encouraged by parliamentarians, well-travelled, and absorbing all that he encountered abroad, Berkeley won permission from George I and a grant of £20,000 from the House of Commons for his Bermuda foundation.

Before setting off he married Anne Forster, daughter of the speaker of the Irish House of Commons and lord chief justice; he also found himself richer by £2,000 from the estate of Esther Van Homrigh, the close friend of Jonathan Swift but estranged from him following a violent disagreement...

[Berkeley] spent three years [in America], mostly in or near Newport, Rhode Island. He did not get to Bermuda – the money from parliament never materialized – but was influential in the educational debates of the day, preached often, wrote and studied. His American sojourn is commemorated in Harvard, Yale, Columbia, and other educational institutions including the University of California [at Berkeley]...

On his appointment to the See of Cloyne [Berkeley] addressed himself to rural poverty, hygiene and ill-health, and produced a best-seller, *Sirus: A Chain of Philosophical Reflexions and Inquiries Concerning the Virtues of Tar-Water* (1744). He and his wife decided to move to Oxford in 1752 to be closer to his son, George, but died there six months later. He is buried in Christ Church, Oxford. Smith [in Charles Smith's *History of Cork* (1750)] offers this contemporary picture of the bishop's time in Cloyne:

"His present Lordship has successfully transplanted the polite arts, which heretofore flourished only in a warmer soil, to this northern climate. Painting and musick are no longer strangers to Ireland, nor confined to Italy. In the Episcopal palace of Cloyne, the eye is entertained with a great variety of good paintings, as well as the ear with concerts of excellent musick. There are here some of the pieces of the best masters, as a Magdalene of Peter Paul Rubens, some heads by Van Dyke and Kneller, besides several good paintings performed in the house, an example so happy that it has diffused itself into the adjacent gentlemen's houses, and there is at present a pleasing emulation raised in this country to vie with each other in these kinds of performances. The great usefulness of Design in the manufactures of stuffs, silks, diapers, damasks, tapestry, embroidery, earthen ware, sculpture, architecture, cabinet work, and an infinite number of other arts is sufficiently evident."

Extract from 'Cloyne' in **The Lie of the Land: Journeys through Literary Cork**, *by Mary Leland (Cork University Press, 1999).*

Ancient Irish Round Tower.

Main Street, Cloyne.　　　*Co. Cork.*

A Lawrence card from the Adrian Healy collection showing the ancient round tower in Cloyne. The tower is believed to date from the time of the monastic settlement founded at Cloyne in the 560s by St Colman. The south coast of Ireland (and Cloyne in particular) was plundered by Norse-men on several occasions in the 9th and 10th centuries (the tower served as a look-out). The postcard was posted in Youghal in August 1905, sent to a Miss Silo at 117 High Street, Hollywood, Co. Down. There is no message.

CHRISTIAN BROTHERS' SCHOOLS, MIDLETON, CO. CORK.

From the John James collection, a Signal Series postcard of the Christian Brothers School in Midleton. Signal Series postcards were produced by E. & S. Publishers of Dublin and Belfast. This postcard was never posted.

I GREW UP in Cloyne, a town where hurling is part of life. There are lots of towns and villages that get tagged with that old cliché. A community that expresses itself through hurling. A place where the game is life and death. A village where religion comes second. And so on…

Like most clichés, the one about Cloyne and hurling fits broadly enough, but it's lazy too, and a little patronizing in the way it bestows a broad simplicity of mind on us all. Life is more complicated than that. We don't live in Cloyne or in Killeagh or in Midleton as a generic tribe of happy folk, content so long as we have ash to swing and leather or rivals to strike.

We have the usual trials and tribulations. We lose our jobs. Our marriages bust up. Our friendships break. Alcohol ruins some of us. Depression follows others like a black dog. We fight. We love. We scar. We heal. We die.

And when we die someone will always say piously that death or illness puts all hurling into perspective, as if our departed comrade had given his life to something trivial and wasteful.

Nobody says it puts it all into perspective when they walk behind the coffin of a dead musician or a dead poet…

I believe hurling is the best of us. One of the greatest and most beautiful expressions of what we can be. For me that is the perspective that death and loss can put on the game. If you could live again you would hurl more, because that is living. You'd pay less attention to the rows and the mortgage and the car and the daily drudge. Hurling is our song and our verse, and when I walk in the graveyard in Cloyne and look at the familiar names on the headstones I know that their owners would want us to hurl with more joy and more exuberance and more (as Frank Murphy used to tell us) abandon than before, because life is shorter than the second half of a tournament game that began at dusk.

From **Come What May: The Autobiography**, by Donal Óg Cusack (Penguin Ireland, 2009).

A Lawrence postcard from the Adrian Healy collection featuring the Presentation Convent in Midleton ('Midleton' because it is the 'middle town' between Cork and Youghal). This postcard was never posted. The Presentation Sisters established themselves in Midleton in the 1830s. The convent was built on a site granted by Lord Midleton and financed by the Coppinger family and the Gould Trust Fund (which had been set up in 1826 for the promotion of Catholic Education in the Diocese of Cloyne). The Primary School opened in 1834 and St Mary's High School in 1902.

A Lawrence postcard from the Adrian Healy collection showing the town square and part of the main street in Midleton. This postcard was never posted. The monument at the centre of the picture is to the men who died in the cause of Irish nationalism.

The College.   Midleton.

A Guy & Company postcard from the John James collection featuring Midleton College boys on the hockey field. Midleton College was founded in 1696 by Elizabeth Villiers, a favourite of King William, housed in a newly constructed handsome limestone building which is still in use today (part of which can be seen in the trees on the left side of the picture). This postcard was never posted. On the picture-side, however, someone has written "Fred" and has an arrow directing attention to one of the boys watching the game in the far distance.

Avoncore Mills Midleton.

From the John James collection, a postcard of Midleton's Avoncore Flour Mills, apparently published by D. Desmond, a Midleton stationer. The card was posted in Midleton in March 1906, to a Mr M.L. Walsh, c/o M. Blake Esq., Patrick Street, Fermoy: "Heard from Kilmagner last evg. I am sure you will be surprised to hear that I played with the Cork Agricultural Team against Macroom – do – on Sunday at Turners Cross. We were beaten by 1 G. 6 pts to nil. I am sore & tired yet as I had no exercise for a very long time. Am writing to wish you well with it – with him. Hope all are good, as ever, Pat."

A "Novelty" postcard from the John James collection. When the flap is opened one finds a concertinaed strip featuring a set of photographic vignettes of Cork: Shandon Church, The Mardyke, St. Finbarres's Cathedral, Blarney Castle, Blackrock Castle, Queenstown Roman Catholic Cathedral, Queenstown Hotel and the Beach, Blackrock and Passage from Queenstown, Queenstown Harbour from Spy Hill, and Queenstwon Harbour. This postcard was never posted – at least, it was never stamped – however, on the B-side the following message is written: "Had a nice time roaming around the city while waiting for train. My Darling XX."